IMAGES
of America

FRANKLIN SQUARE

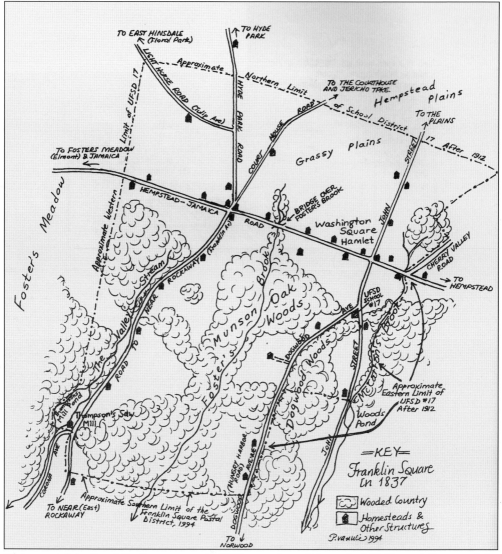

This map of the Franklin Square area in 1837 was adapted from the US Coastal Survey of the same year. It is evident that Franklin Square was a sparsely populated rural area with no village center. Much of the land, especially north of Hempstead Turnpike, was open, grassy land—part of the Hempstead Plains. Woodland tended to cluster around the small brooks that drained the countryside. The map was drawn in 1994 by Franklin Square historian Paul van Wie. (Courtesy of the Franklin Square Historical Society.)

ON THE COVER: The Rath family, one of the founding families of Franklin Square, arrived from Germany in the 19th century. In the early 20th century, they lived in this home on Madison Avenue, just north of Hempstead Turnpike. John Rath, after whom Rath Park is named, is the boy at right. To his left are his siblings Raymond and Annette; his mother and grandmother stand on the porch. (Courtesy of the Franklin Square Historical Society.)

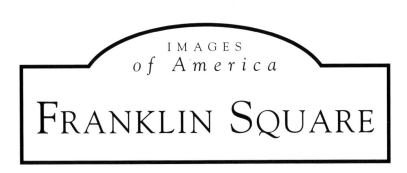

IMAGES
of America

FRANKLIN SQUARE

Paul van Wie, PhD, Kiera Grassi,
and Hannah Mutum

ARCADIA
PUBLISHING

Copyright © 2011 by Franklin Square Historical Society
ISBN 978-0-7385-7589-6

Published by Arcadia Publishing
Charleston, South Carolina

Printed in the United States of America

Library of Congress Control Number: 2011921505

For all general information, please contact Arcadia Publishing:
Telephone 843-853-2070
Fax 843-853-0044
E-mail sales@arcadiapublishing.com
For customer service and orders:
Toll-Free 1-888-313-2665

Visit us on the Internet at www.arcadiapublishing.com

CONTENTS

ACKNOWLEDGMENTS

In 1975, Franklin Square's history was in danger of being lost and dispersed. The generations born in the late 19th and early 20th centuries were rapidly passing from the scene. Before it was too late, a small committee began the task of collecting our community's history. We interviewed members of the "old" families and in the process discovered their family albums and photographs. Over 100 photographs were carefully copied and identified, and within a year the nucleus of a collection had been assembled. In 1979, the Franklin Square Historical Society was formally organized to continue the work. Today, the society has over 2,000 photographs, hundreds of unique artifacts, and a museum—currently under construction—that will preserve these materials for generations to come. Unless otherwise noted, all images appear courtesy of the Franklin Square Historical Society.

All of us are indebted to the society for their ongoing work, perseverance, and volunteer spirit. Elizabeth McIsaac, vice president of the Franklin Square Historical Society, deserves special thanks for her assistance in the preparation of this book. Elizabeth exemplifies the energetic and determined Franklin Square spirit. Carol Grassi and Doreen Mutum provided unending encouragement, advice, and expertise in the production of this work. Without their support, the book would not have been possible. In addition, the van Wie family has lent patient support (and storage space) for over 35 years for many of these pictures.

We cannot forget to acknowledge Kathleen Murphy and the Girl Scouts of Nassau County. It was the Girl Scouts of Nassau County who inspired Kiera Grassi and Hannah Mutum to work on their Gold Awards by taking action in their community. The Girl Scout Gold Award requires Girl Scouts to find a sustainable project in their community that they deeply care about. The work on their Girl Scout Gold Award with their project advisor, Dr. van Wie, led them to the idea of collaborating with him on this book. And the rest, as they say, is history.

Lastly, we would like to thank the many neighbors and community members who generously lent photographs and materials for inclusion in this book. We thank you for your enthusiasm and assistance because in a very real sense the story told in this book is your own story.

INTRODUCTION

Franklin Square is a suburban community of nearly 30,000 people located in Nassau County, Long Island, New York.

A microcosm of American history, Franklin Square has experienced the colonial Dutch and English culture, the upheavals of the American Revolution, the economic growth of the 19th century, the waves of European immigration, the rise of the automobile culture and aviation, and the sweeping suburbanization of the 20th century. Throughout Franklin Square's existence, the proximity of the nation's largest city, New York City, has exerted a powerful influence.

The village of Franklin Square first developed in the 19th century. Immigrants from southern and western Germany purchased land in the locality, transforming Franklin Square into lush vegetable farms oriented toward the New York City market. Franklin Square remained a German-speaking farming village until the 1920s. As an ethnic enclave, the community developed its own distinctive traditions that endure to this day.

In the 1860s, a small hotel was built at the corner of New Hyde Park Road and Hempstead Turnpike. This hotel, which endured until 1923, was owned by the Kalb family for several decades. A social and business center with a dance hall, restaurant, and bowling alley, the hotel became the nucleus of the village. In 1902, the Hempstead Turnpike trolley was extended through Franklin Square and within several years the first residential subdivision was laid out. A group of farmers initiated the first volunteer fire company in 1907. In 1908, the predominantly Roman Catholic townspeople organized Franklin Square's first religious congregation, St. Catherine of Sienna Church. In 1912, a new brick schoolhouse was constructed on Monroe Street in the heart of the original residential area.

Franklin Square's transition from farming village to suburban neighborhood began in the early 1920s. Between 1920 and 1930, hundreds of homes were constructed on the side streets just off Hempstead Turnpike. This rapid growth ended abruptly with the stock market crash of 1929 and the ensuing Depression. The situation was temporary, however, because Franklin Square's advantageous location and convenience to New York City assured a bustling future. Between 1937 and 1942, a second building boom transformed the eastern and southern sections of Franklin Square. During these years, Franklin Square was one of the fastest-growing communities in the United States. World War II temporarily interrupted this explosive growth, but after the end of the war, home construction rapidly resumed. Between 1946 and 1953, the remaining farms along Dogwood Avenue were subdivided into housing developments and almost no open space was left in the village.

The Franklin Square National Bank, founded in 1926 and later known as Franklin National Bank, rapidly accelerated growth in the town. The bank began as a small hometown institution where the staff knew each customer by name. It grew very slowly at first and almost failed during the depths of the Depression. Then, in 1934, Arthur Roth was hired to run the bank's daily operations. Roth has been described as one of the most important figures in the history of

American banking. He built the bank into one of the largest financial institutions in the United States through a series of brilliant innovations. Roth developed the first bank walk-up window, the Franklin Square bank had the first bank parking lot anywhere, and the Franklin National Bank invented the bank credit card, which changed business practices forever. In the mid-20th century, Franklin Square's bank financed much of the housing construction on Long Island.

As an unincorporated village, Franklin Square has often been defined by its school system, District 17. The famous American poet Walt Whitman taught in the original schoolhouse in 1840. Between 1912 and 1956, Franklin Square citizens built and financed four substantial public elementary schools, a junior-senior high school, and a K-8 Catholic school. These institutions and their reputations for quality education remain a source of great pride.

Though Franklin Square has a population of nearly 30,000, it has maintained the ambiance of a small village. Franklin Square is indeed small in area—perhaps two miles by two miles—but with a fairly dense population. Neighbors get to know one another, if only because they live in close proximity. Families remain in Franklin Square, and often in the same house, for generations. A variety of organizations serve to reinforce community ties, including athletic leagues, religious groups, charitable organizations, the PTA, civic groups, the fire department, the historical society, and veterans' organizations. Many residents are able to walk to stores, banks, church, and the post office. Small specialty shops predominate in the old-fashioned downtown area. Many of these shops cater to the tastes of Franklin Square's vibrant Italian American community, the largest ethnic group in the village.

Franklin Square residents value the quiet atmosphere and attractive tree-lined residential streets that are the essence of the community. To its residents, Franklin Square is simply home. With this in mind, we present this volume on Franklin Square—a pictorial record of an American hometown with its own unique history.

One

RURAL HERITAGE

In the 21st century, it is hard to imagine Franklin Square as a rural community. Until the 1920s, however, it was a farming village full of open space, farms, fields, and woods. Small creeks flowed through the center of town, providing opportunities for fishing, swimming, and recreation. Just a century ago, there was no electricity or street lighting and residents walked around with lanterns at night. Water came from a hand pump in the kitchen, and wood or coal stoves provided heat. Beginning in 1902, a trolley on Hempstead Turnpike connected Franklin Square to Jamaica and Hempstead. Until 1915, most families depended on horses for transportation.

Franklin Square was well known for the produce of its fertile farms. Most farms grew vegetables for the New York City market—potatoes, cabbage, corn, beets, horseradish, spinach, asparagus, string beans, and tomatoes. Farmlands ranged from a few acres to the large Hoffman farm, which stretched from Hempstead Turnpike to Naple Avenue and from Franklin Avenue to Rath Park.

Between 1922 and 1953, Franklin Square made the transition from a rural community to a suburban town. Three building booms, from 1923 to 1929, 1937 to 1942, and 1946 to 1953, resulted in subdivisions of one-family homes. By the middle of the 1950s, there was almost no remaining open space in Franklin Square. Luckily, John Rath encouraged the Town of Hempstead to preserve acres for a park, and so today the town is fortunate to have Rath Park.

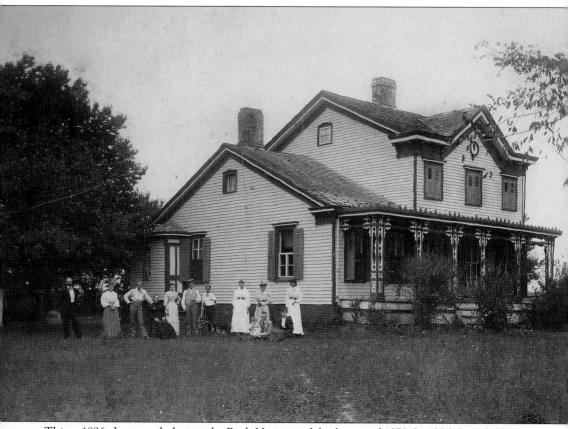

This c. 1896 photograph depicts the Rath Homestead, built around 1870. In 1896, Peter J. Herman and his wife, Catherine Rath, moved into the house. They lived there until the house burned down on March 10, 1901, at midnight. The homestead was located at the west corner of Hempstead Turnpike and Herman Boulevard. The seated elderly woman is believed to be Annette Katherine Rath, mother-in-law of Peter J. Herman and grandmother of John E. Rath.

Antoinette DiBella (right) and her sister Adeline Campanella tend a vegetable garden at the DiBella's property on Third Avenue in 1942. Note the wide open farmland in the background; southern Franklin Square was not built up until the early 1950s. Though the Italian American families in the Third Avenue neighborhood were avid gardeners, the food shortages of the World War II era gave special urgency to DiBella and Campanella's work. (Courtesy of Lori Wallach.)

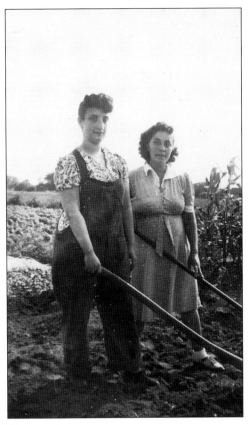

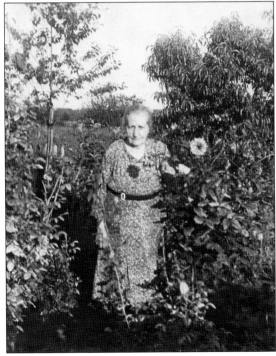

In an image from the early 1940s, Maria DiCosta Tornese stands in the midst of her gardens at the family property on Second Avenue. Tornese was one of many Italian American immigrants who settled in the Gardenia Park development. At this time, Gardenia Park was largely summer bungalows and vegetable gardens tended by families who lived in the city. (Courtesy of Lori Wallach.)

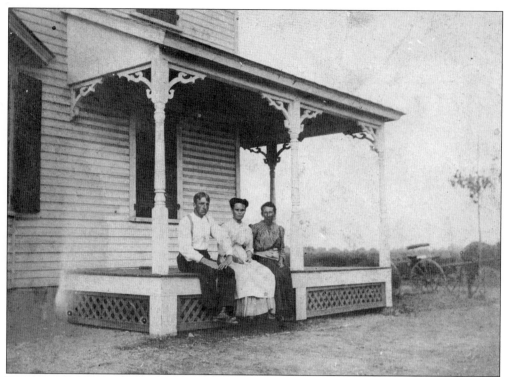

In this c. 1912 photograph, the Gaynor family relaxes on the side porch of their home (today's 119 Court House Road). At rear is the family's horse and buggy, parked on Court House Road. Note the open fields beyond. The Gaynor family occupied this home for nearly a century and was active in community life.

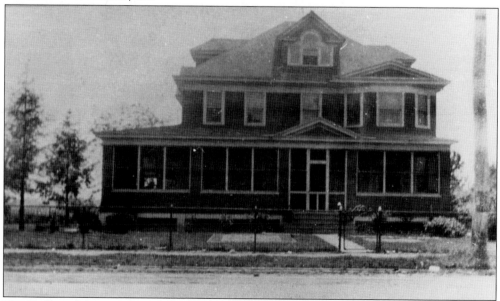

The Hoffman homestead, located on the south side of Hempstead Turnpike, west of James Street, was called the mansion by local people. It was built in the early 1900s and was surrounded by fine grounds. This photograph was taken about 1925, and the house was razed around 1937.

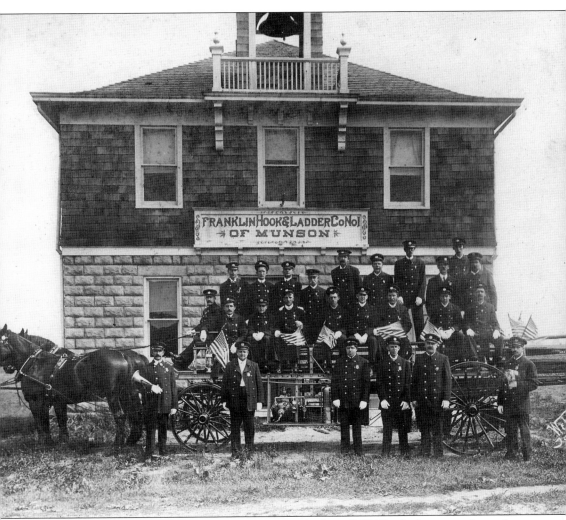

This is an early picture of the old Munson Fire House, built in 1907. The firehouse was located on Hempstead Turnpike between Poppy and McKinley Avenues. This view dates from about 1913. The sign reads, "Franklin Hook and Ladder Co. No. 1 of Munson." Note the horse-drawn wagon, which was purchased in 1908 and remained in service until 1922. The fire bell was from the old Munson schoolhouse on Nassau Boulevard. The fire company purchased the bell when the school closed in 1912. In the early years, many of the fires this group responded to were grass fires on the open plains north of town. In the 1920s, the Munson group merged with the Franklin Square volunteer fire company to form the Franklin Square and Munson Fire Department. Their current headquarters is located on Liberty Place, just a few blocks south of the old Munson Firehouse.

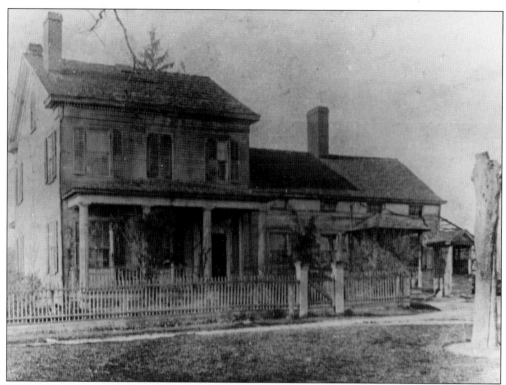

This is the home of Elnathan Eldert, located on Franklin Avenue opposite the area now occupied by Garden World. This colonial home, built in the 1700s, was said to be the oldest building in Franklin Square. It was one of Franklin Square's links with colonial times. The building was razed about 1940; this photograph was taken shortly before the house was razed.

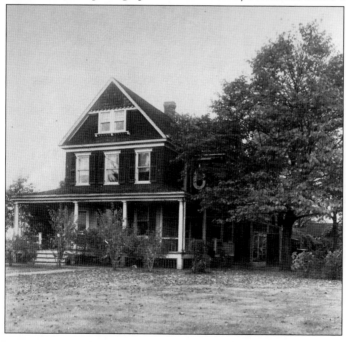

The Peter J. Herman House, located on the north side of Hempstead Turnpike at Herman Boulevard, had broad lawns sloping down to the turnpike. The house was built in 1901 by Carl Mirschel and was later moved to the corner of Herman Boulevard and Lloyd Street. This view dates from about 1910. This home had the first indoor plumbing in the village.

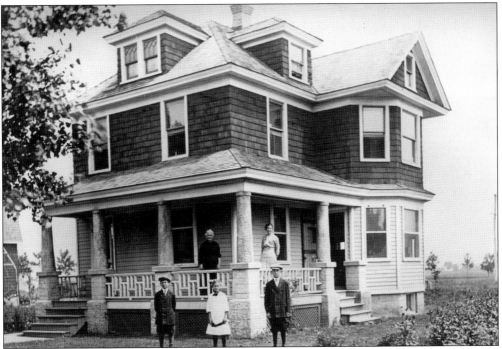

This c. 1912 photograph shows the Rath home on Madison Avenue in Franklin Square. The home was located just north of the Hempstead Turnpike on the east side of the street. Built around 1910, it was razed in the 1970s. In the photograph are three Rath children, Raymond (left), Annette (center), and John. Their mother and grandmother stand on the porch.

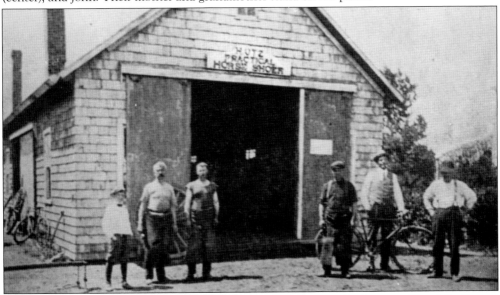

Herman Utz's blacksmith shop, pictured here around 1915, was a focal point of Franklin Square life in the early 20th century. Herman Utz was a farmer and board of education president who shoed horses and fixed bicycles, wheels, tools, and agricultural implements. This building was located just west of the present entrance to the Franklin Square firehouse on Hempstead Turnpike, not far from the brook.

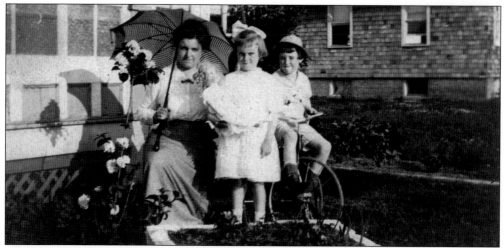

The Quinn family posed in front of their home at 114 Monroe Street in this photograph taken on June 18, 1916. From left to right, they are Ethel, Helen (born 1909), and Harrison Quinn (born 1910). The Quinns moved into their newly built home in August 1913. At rear is the St. James Episcopal Mission, which was constructed the year before this picture was taken.

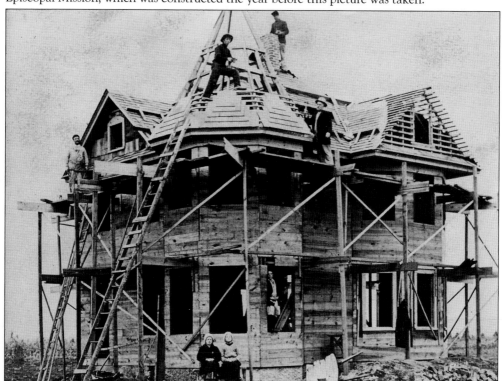

This c. 1905 photograph depicts the Mott-Schoenlein house under construction. The house is located at the northeastern corner of Madison Avenue and Roosevelt Street. It was built by the Mott family c. 1905 and sold to the Schoenlein family in 1920. This was the first residential house in the whole surrounding section. Pictured here are, from left to right, Mr. Combes, Jim Mott Jr., Oscar Mott, Jim Mott Sr., and three unidentified. Note the cornfields surrounding the house at harvest time.

One of the Gaynor children stands on the sidewalk near the front of his home in this picture from around 1912. The view is looking north on Court House Road toward present-day Garfield Street. Note the open fields at right and the barn on the horizon; fields in the foreground were part of the former Kreischer farm.

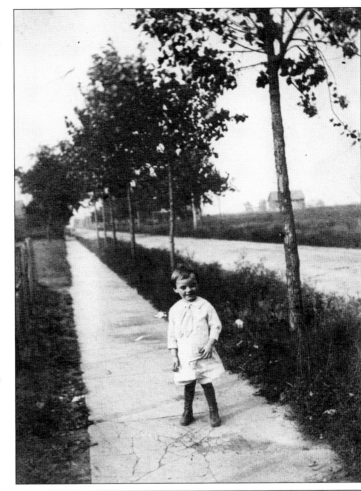

This photograph, taken on October 1, 1950, offers a good perspective of the construction of Forte Homes. The view is from Marion Street and Forte Boulevard. This photograph exemplifies the massive development that occurred from 1946 to 1955 in the southern areas of Franklin Square.

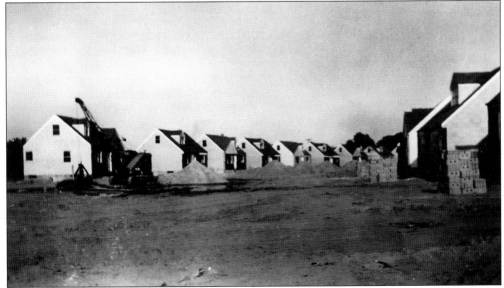

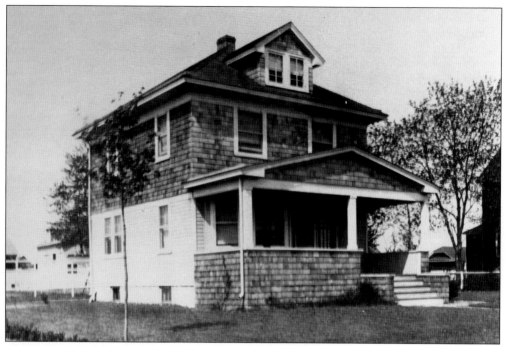

The fine home of James W. Randell Jr. was located on Hempstead Turnpike at the east corner of Lexington Avenue. The house dates from about 1917, and this photograph was taken in 1920. In the early 20th century, Hempstead Turnpike was lined with one-family homes.

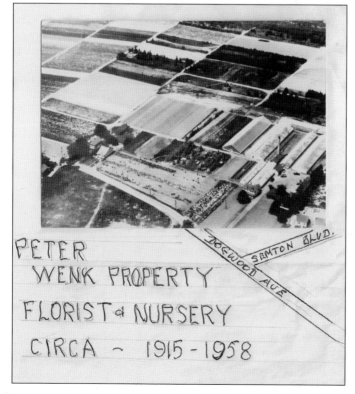

PETER WENK PROPERTY FLORIST & NURSERY CIRCA ~ 1915-1958

The Wenk farm, which included a florist and nursery business, was located on Dogwood Avenue, just south of Semton Boulevard. Peter Wenk and his family operated the farm from about 1915 until the property was sold in 1958. In this bird's-eye-view image from about 1945, Dogwood Avenue is visible at lower left. At lower right is the Wenk farmhouse. This type of landscape dominated lower Dogwood Avenue until the early 1950s when the farms were subdivided.

In 1916, seven-year-old Helen Quinn (left) and her brother Harrison, age six, posed for this picture while dressed as Indians for a school pageant. The view, looking north toward Garfield Street, is from the yard of their home at 114 Monroe Street. Note the open expanse of land, which had been used as farmland until a year or two before this photograph was taken.

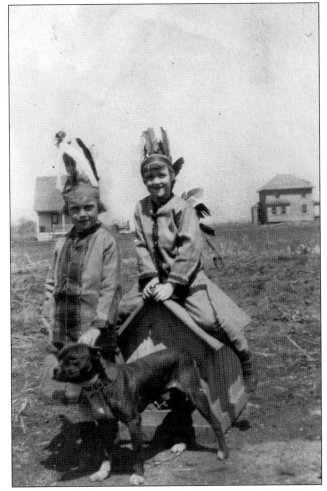

This April 1954 picture, taken during spring planting, depicts the Wolf farm, located on the east side of New Hyde Park Road near Tulip Avenue. The northward view shows the outbuildings and the barn. The Wolf farm had a fine set of outbuildings, as seen here, including chicken coops, wood and tool sheds, and more.

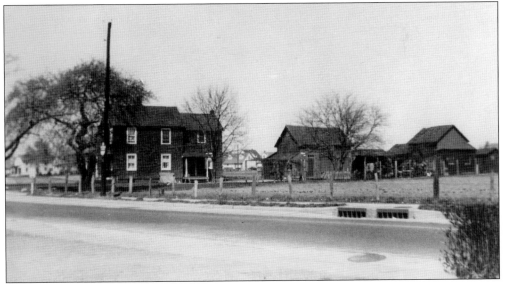

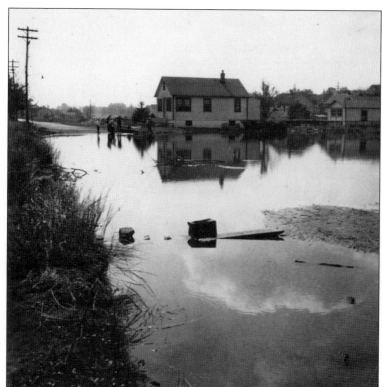

This view of McKinley Avenue near Garfield Street dates from 1949. The view is looking south on McKinley Avenue. The pond in the foreground was a result of temporary flooding. This area was called the Hollow. The Hollow had poor drainage and a high water table. Such conditions inhibited home building in the immediate vicinity. Until sewers were installed in the 1950s, flooding was a common sight.

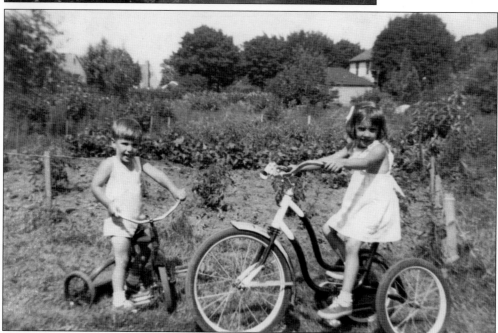

This photograph, dating from around 1951, shows Herbert and Susan Barber in front of a vacant lot at 917 Stewart Place. The photograph was taken from their home at 921 Stewart Place. Stewart Place was in the traditionally Italian section of Franklin Square, often called "Little Italy," and the Mount Carmel Hall was near this site.

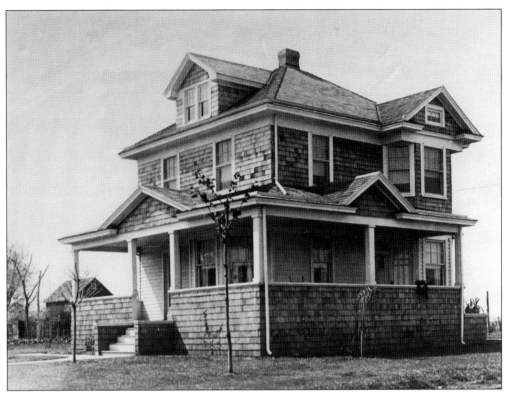

The large home of Herman Utz is the subject of this photograph. His house was located on the north side of Hempstead Turnpike and the west corner of Lexington Avenue. Behind the home were his fields, visible at far right. Note the shed at left. Like the Randell house, the Utz house no longer stands; stores have replaced them on the busy turnpike.

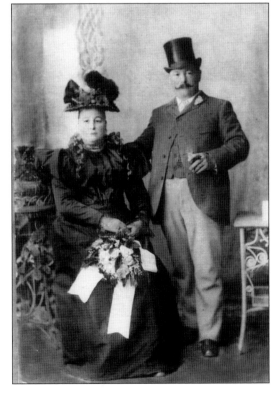

This wedding picture of Catherine Kreischer and August Kalb was taken on September 5, 1882. The couple was married at St. Boniface's Church in Elmont and settled in Franklin Square, where they operated the well-known Kalb Hotel. By the early 21st century, the Kalb family had lived in Franklin Square for seven generations.

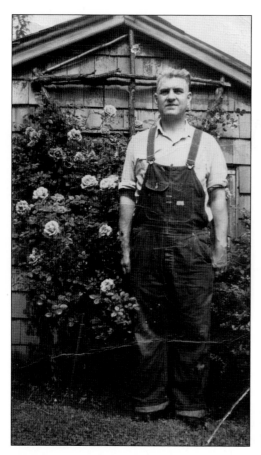

Arthur Wenzig proudly displays some of his gardening talents in this photograph dating from the 1940s. The Wenzig home was located on the east side of Franklin Avenue near Arlington Avenue. At one point, the Wenzigs operated a gas station on the adjacent property.

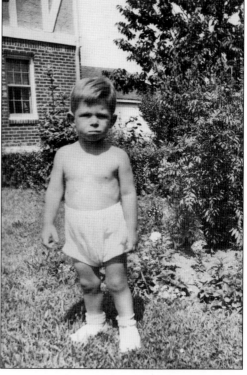

Artie Weinberg, a longtime Franklin Square resident, stands in his aunt's garden on Fendale Street in this 1942 photograph. This area of Franklin Square was quite new that year. Weinberg grew up to raise his own family in Franklin Square and is still an active member in many community organizations, including the Carey Dads' Club. (Courtesy of Artie Weinberg.)

Two

MINDING OUR BUSINESS

The beginning of the business district of Franklin Square can be traced to the two small hotels built at Hempstead Turnpike and New Hyde Park Road in the mid-1800s. By 1900, the larger of these two hotels, the Kalb Hotel, did a thriving business. The Kalb Hotel contained a dining room, a saloon, overnight accommodations, a dance hall, and a bowling alley, as well as spacious barns and an outdoor picnic area. It was a center of local life and attracted people on excursions from the big city.

By the early 20th century, Franklin Square boasted a dry goods store, a grocery store, a butcher, and a barbershop. In the 1920s, bakeries, lumberyards, vegetable stores, and Schilling's Hardware Store joined these early businesses. Supermarkets arrived in the 1940s, and today there are hundreds of businesses in Franklin Square.

The most famous business in Franklin Square, the Franklin Square National Bank (later known as Franklin National Bank), opened in a storefront in 1926. Beginning with capital of only $50,000, the bank originally had just three employees. Just as the bank was beginning to grow, the stock market crashed in 1929 and kicked off the Great Depression. The local economy suffered, and the bank was on the verge of collapse. In 1934, a young banker named Arthur Roth was hired to run the bank; his energy and ideas saved it. As time passed, Roth helped the Franklin National Bank grow into one of the largest financial institutions in the United States. Roth transformed American banking with his innovations—Franklin National was the first bank to have a walk-up window and a parking lot and it invented the bank credit card. Significantly, the Franklin National Bank helped to finance the dramatic growth of Nassau and Suffolk Counties after World War II. After being sold to foreign interests, the bank went through the largest collapse in American history (up until that time) in 1974.

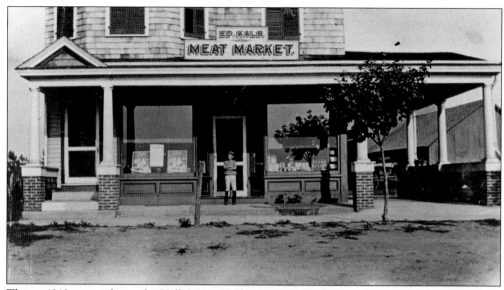

This c. 1910 image shows the Kalb Meat Market on New Hyde Park Road. Edward Kalb, son of Kalb Hotel owner August Kalb, ran the meat market until Max Thomala bought the business in 1914. Note the Kalb Hotel horse barn at right. It was later moved and renovated and eventually became the St. Catherine of Sienna Church parish hall.

The Washington Market, located on Hempstead Turnpike near New Hyde Park Road, was a popular grocery store for many years. This advertisement from 1940 reflects the prevailing prices of the day. However, food was anything but cheap for a citizenry only just emerging from the Great Depression. By the 1950s, modern supermarkets had replaced many of these small grocery stores.

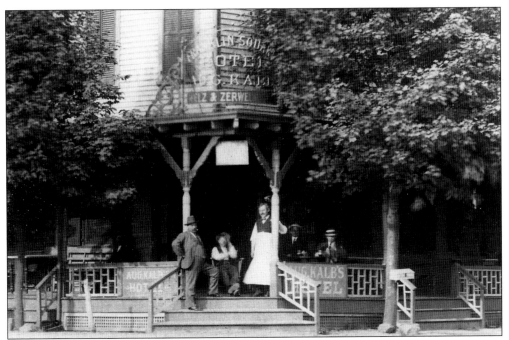

The Kalb Hotel, located at New Hyde Park Road and Hempstead Turnpike, was the center of community life and a popular destination for excursions from Brooklyn until it burned down in early 1923. Owner August Kalb is seen above around 1910 in his white apron.

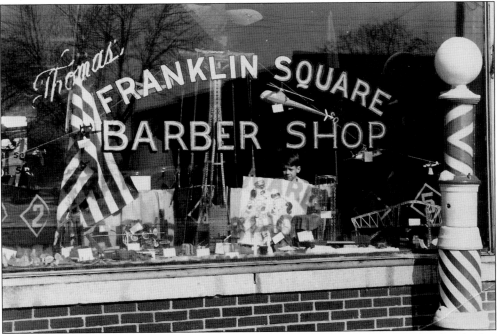

A Cub Scout window display of the early 1950s is the subject of this photograph taken by Jim Fitchett of Jefferson Street. Thomas' Franklin Square Barber Shop was located at 952 Hempstead Turnpike, between New Hyde Park Road and Franklin Street. A barbershop has operated in that location since at least the 1930s.

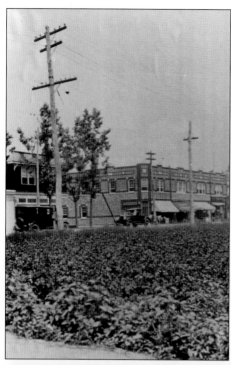

This photograph depicts downtown Franklin Square as it appeared in 1924. The building at left is Schilling's, and the one at right is the Laibach Building; both are still standing and occupied with tenants. The potato field in the foreground was owned by the Hoffmans and was later the site of the Franklin Square National Bank building, constructed in 1929.

This photograph shows the interior of the J and G Service gas station, located at Harrison Avenue and Hempstead Turnpike, on December 19, 1949. The picture was taken after a robbery, when the premises were considered a crime scene.

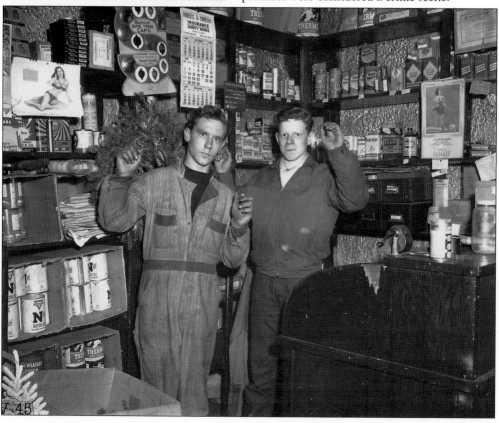

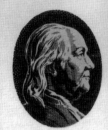

With
THIS CREDIT CARD BOOKLET
You Can . . .

- "CHARGE IT!" at any of the hundreds of Franklin Credit Card Member Stores listed inside or displaying the Franklin Credit Card emblem (frozen food purchases subject to special arrangements).

- CHARGE CASH! Just present this Credit Card at any Franklin office, sign for the money you need (up to $100.) and walk away with the cash!

FRANKLIN NATIONAL BANK
Member FDIC

In the 1950s, the Franklin National Bank initiated an ingenious new idea: the bank credit card. Franklin was the first bank in the United States to have such a program. Shown here is the credit card—really a booklet—that the customer displayed when purchasing an item.

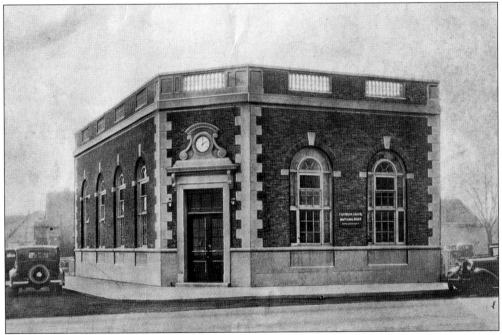

This photograph of the Franklin Square National Bank building dates from about 1930, the year when the structure was formally opened for business. The bank, founded in 1926, opened the building just as the Great Depression began. The building was enlarged many times (in 1939, 1946, and 1955) as the bank grew. The street in the foreground is Hempstead Turnpike; at left is James Street.

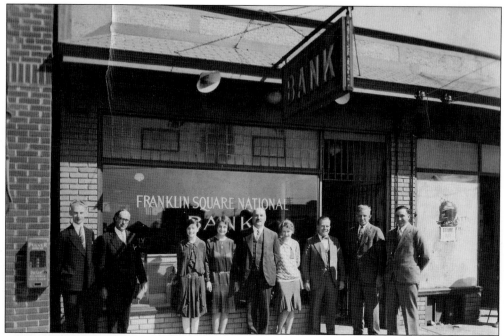

The Franklin Square National Bank, founded by local businessmen Arthur C. Phillips and Fred Schilling, opened its doors in 1926. The bank's original quarters were at 334 Hempstead Turnpike. Pictured at the original bank in 1929 are, from left to right, R. Johnson, J. Laux, E. Smith, Katherine Rauch, Phillips, Dorothy McKenna, cashier Lloyd Flint, Schilling, and Herbert Mirschel.

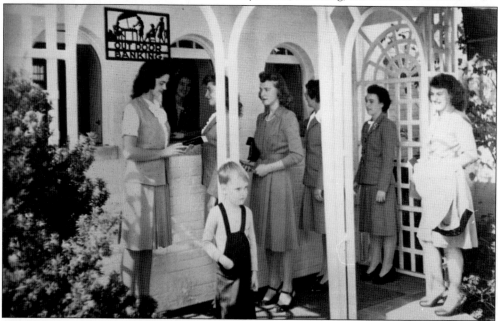

This c. 1945 photograph offers a unique view of the outdoor banking facility of the Franklin Square National Bank. The facility was located on the west side of James Street just south of Hempstead Turnpike. Note the decorative touches in this facility designed to appeal to female customers; a live bird was part of the decor.

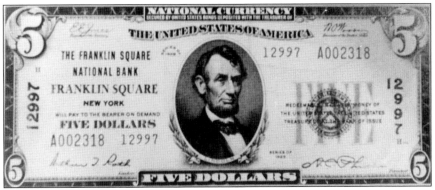

The Franklin Square National Bank was accorded the privilege of issuing its own paper money (subject to the regulations of the federal government). This photograph of a Franklin National Bank $5 bill clearly shows the village and the bank's names. Note the double set of signatures; the bottom set includes cashier Arthur T. Roth and president Arthur C. Phillips.

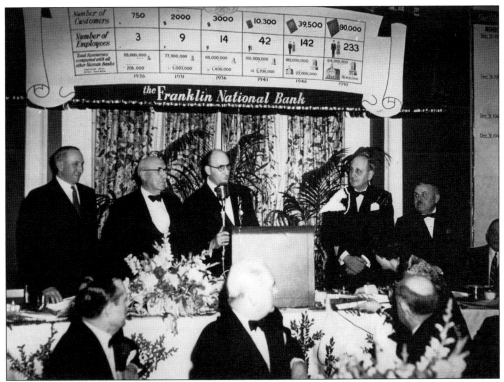

In 1951, the Franklin National Bank celebrated its silver anniversary with a gala dinner at the Garden City Hotel. At the dais on the auspicious occasion were, from left to right, director Herbert Mirschel, first bank president Arthur C. Phillips, president Arthur T. Roth, director George Estabrook, and director Leo Laibach. Note the charts at the top of the photograph, which proudly document the bank's dramatic growth.

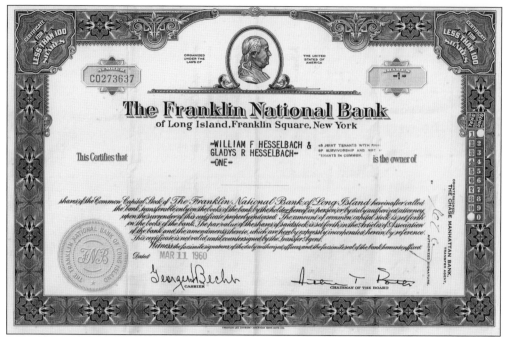

This stock certificate was issued by the Franklin National Bank in 1960. In 1949, the Franklin Square National Bank dropped the "Square" from its name to assist its transition to "a larger sphere of operations." Indeed, by the mid-1960s, Franklin Square's hometown bank had become one of the largest in the United States. Note the bust of Benjamin Franklin on the certificate; this design was the symbol of the bank.

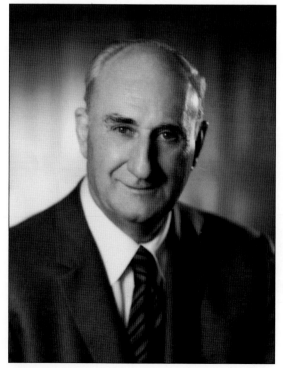

Arthur T. Roth (1905–1997), the son of immigrants from Mainaschaff, Bavaria, was the genius behind the Franklin National Bank's rise to national greatness. Roth has been described as one of the three greatest figures in the American banking industry, and he was one of the most important personalities in the development of Franklin Square. His career at the bank ended in 1968.

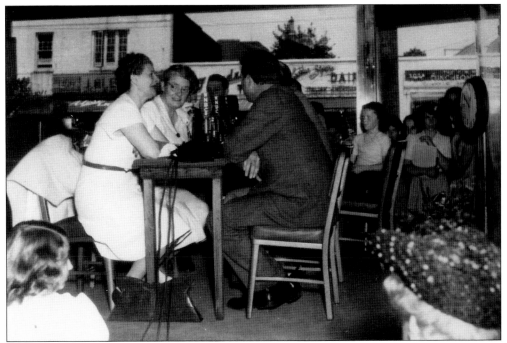

On June 21, 1947, a live radio broadcast was held in the consumer lobby of the Franklin Square National Bank as part of the dedication festivities for the new building. Mary Margaret McBride hosted her popular show on this day, and in this picture she is shown interviewing guests. Publicity efforts such as this radio show garnered nationwide publicity for the bank.

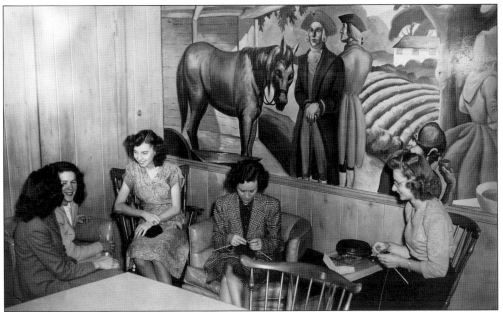

Employees of the Franklin Square National Bank enjoy a break in the building's basement recreation room around 1948. Note the Colonial-style mural and furniture. The lunch table is in the foreground. Janet Smith is pictured fourth from the left, knitting; the other women are unidentified. The bank's policies emphasized employee morale and teamwork.

FIRE BOXES

Know the Call Box Nearest Your Home

No. 211—Fire Headquarters
No. 212—Monroe Street School
No. 213—Hempstead Turnpike and New Hyde Park Road
No. 214—Randolph St. & Phoebe St.
No. 216—Old Folks' Home
No. 221—Garfield St. & Harrison Ave.
No. 223—Pacific St. & Maxwell St.
No. 224—Lexington Ave. & Lawrence St.
No. 232—Madison Ave. & Washington St.
No. 233—New Hyde Park Road and Washington St.
No. 235—Herman Blvd. & Barnes St.
No. 245—Roosevelt Ave. & Benmore Ave.
No. 252—Court House Road & King's Court
No. 254—New Hyde Park Road and Cathedral Ave.
No. 311—Munson Fire House

No. 313—Hempstead Turnpike and Wellington Road
No. 321—Goldenrod Ave. & Garfield St.
No. 342—Harvard Rd. & 1st Place
No. 345—Brixton Rd. & Ardsley Blvd.
No. 354—Nassau Blvd. & Princeton Rd.
No. 412—Jefferson St. & Benris Ave.
No. 415—Scherer Blvd. & Rosegold St.
No. 416—Catherine Ave. & Russell St.
No. 423—Fenworth Blvd. & Hoffman St.
No. 424—Franklin Ave. & Theodora St.
No. 432—Madison St. & Naple Ave.
No. 435—Franklin Ave. & Norbray St.
No. 444—Lincoln Ave. & Van Buren St.
No. 512—Fendale St. & Benris Ave.
No. 514—John Street School
No. 521—Commonwealth St. and Fenworth Blvd.
No. 552—Dogwood Ave. near Miller Bros.

After the establishment of the Franklin Square and Munson Fire Department in 1924, fire alarm boxes were placed throughout the residential areas of Franklin Square. In those days, when a fire broke out, it was necessary to run to the alarm box to alert the fire department. Even though this was time-consuming, the system was better than the old alarm bell or gong used in the early 1900s. This list dates from 1942.

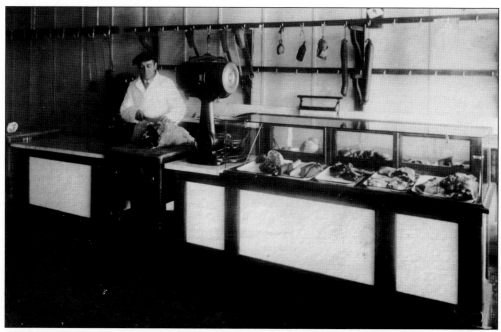

This c. 1910 photograph shows Edward Kalb inside his New Hyde Park Road meat market. Edward was the son of August Kalb, owner of the adjoining hotel. Note the array of fresh meat and homemade wursts on Kalb's counter. In 1914, Max Thomala bought the meat market, and he operated it into the 1950s.

In the 1940s, Franklin Square resident Trudy Marshall was signed to a Hollywood movie contract. Before departing for California, Trudy was given a grand send-off at the Franklin Theater. In this photograph from 1945, the marquee of the Franklin Theater can be seen on Hempstead Turnpike, looking east. Marshall's film, *The Sullivans*, was playing and local pride dictated that she be given top billing.

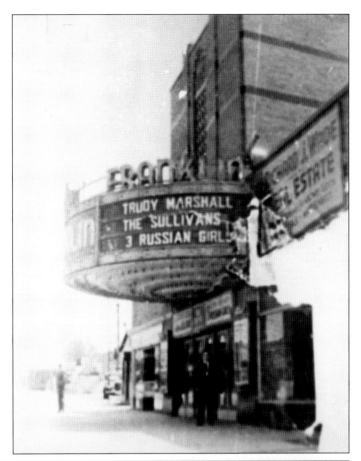

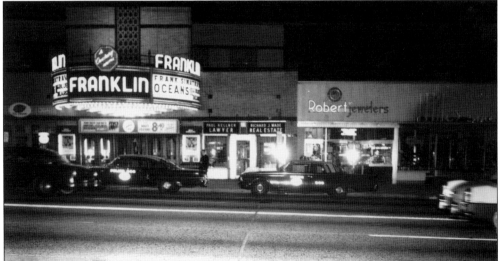

This nighttime view of the Franklin Theater dates from November 1960. The Franklin was built in 1931, and its original round marquee is still visible in this photograph; a rectangular one was installed in the 1960s. The photograph was taken from the north side of Hempstead Turnpike, looking south. Note Robert Jewelers, a long-surviving business, to the right of the theater.

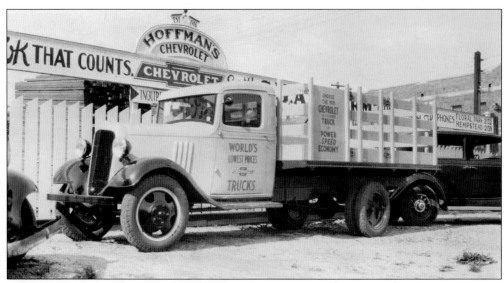

A 1935 Chevrolet truck is the subject of this May 1935 photograph taken at the used car lot at Hoffman Chevrolet, located at the northwest corner of Hempstead Turnpike and New Hyde Park Road. Notice the sign reminding the reader that the business was founded in 1916. Behind the picket fence is the Franklin Square lumberyard.

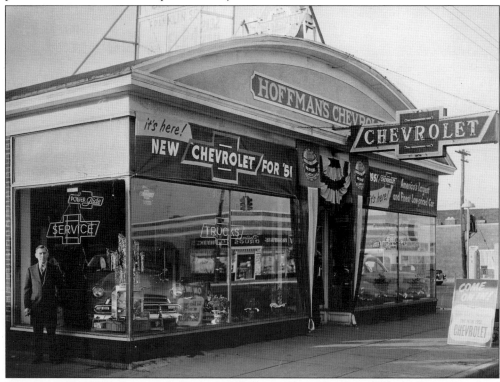

This December 1950 photograph shows the Hoffman Chevrolet showroom on the south side of Hempstead Turnpike, just east of Franklin Avenue. The building was constructed in 1916 as the Hoffman Garage. At the far left in this picture is George Hoffman Sr., proprietor of Hoffman Chevrolet. This site of this picture is presently occupied by Astoria Federal Savings.

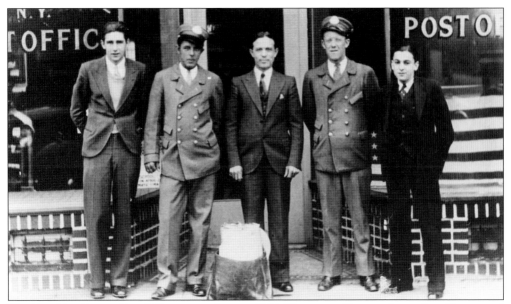

The Franklin Square Post Office is seen here in 1929. This post office was located on Hempstead Turnpike in a storefront near James Street. Shown are, from left to right, Herman Ruge, clerk; John Morton, letter carrier; postmaster Joseph Alese; Sam Hume, letter carrier; and E.H. Kalb, assistant postmaster for many years.

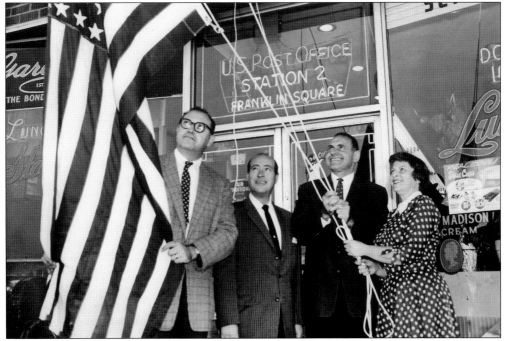

Around 1961, the Franklin Square Post Office opened a substation in the southernmost area of the postal district. The substation was located in a stationery store on Franklin Avenue at Palermo Court. In this photograph taken on the opening day of the substation, the flag is being raised. Congressman John Wydler is at far left, while Franklin Square postmaster Jack Nicastri holds the rope. The other two people are unidentified.

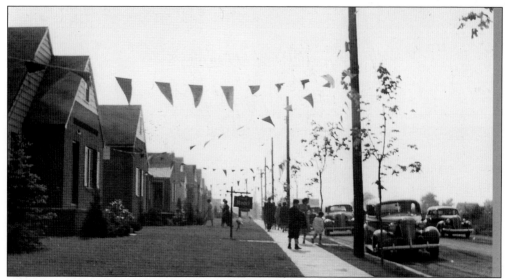

In the late 1930s, as economic conditions slowly improved, many housing developments began. Many of these homes were built on the southern side of Franklin Square, within three blocks of Hempstead Turnpike. One of the developments of this era was Miller Homes, shown in this picture taken somewhere near Scherer Boulevard east of Franklin Avenue in 1939 or 1940. These model homes attracted crowds on weekends.

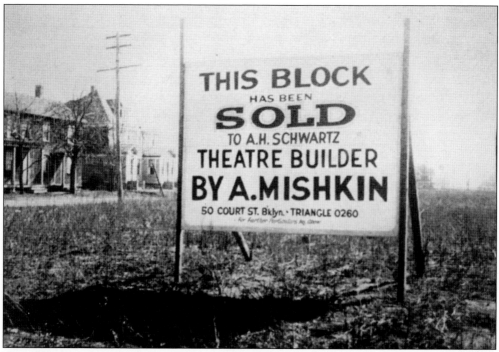

This 1925 photograph shows the west corner of Franklin Square Avenue and Hempstead Turnpike. At that time, the former Kinsey Estate was being subdivided into a development called Franklin Square Gardens. The Franklin Square Theater was completed six years later on this site. The picture gives a good indication of the undeveloped nature of Franklin Square—even the downtown area—in 1925.

36

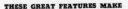
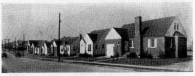

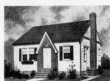
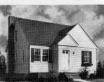
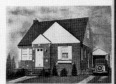

In the late 1930s, home building resumed once more in Franklin Square after ceasing during the Great Depression. One of the housing developments from this era was Franklin Homes, located generally east of Scherer Boulevard and south of Hempstead Turnpike. This 1941 advertisement displays the various models available, beginning at $3,777. The development proved to be popular with home buyers. (Courtesy of Tom O'Grady.)

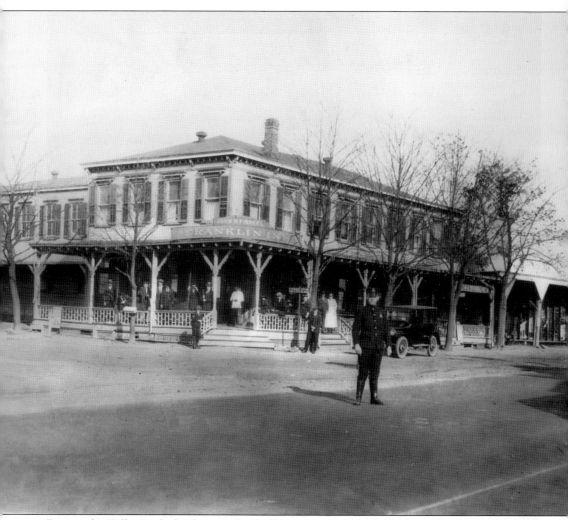

During the Kalb Hotel's final years, the business was run by John and Katie Fischer on behalf of the owner, Jacob Hoffman. The Fischers renamed the establishment the Franklin Inn, though local residents (and subsequent generations) always refer to it as Kalb's. This photograph dates from around 1920, three years before the hotel was destroyed in a spectacular fire one winter's night. The fire was so intense that the heat melted the hoses at Hoffman's Garage across the street. By 1920, Sunday traffic had grown to the point that the services of Constable John McKinley (pictured at center) were needed, as there were not yet traffic lights. Note the trolley tracks on Hempstead Turnpike.

For many years, Peter Meyer of James Street ran a moving and trucking business. This charming photograph from the 1930s was taken in the yard of Meyer's company off Hempstead Turnpike. Peter and his wife, Eleanor, remained in Franklin Square for their entire adult lives, working ceaselessly for the fire department, St. Catherine of Sienna Church, and a number of other civic organizations.

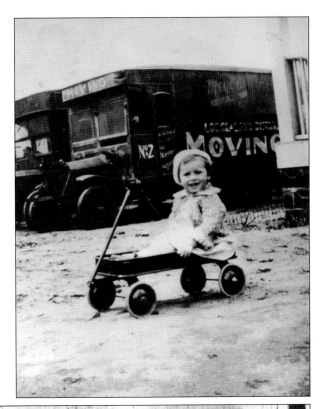

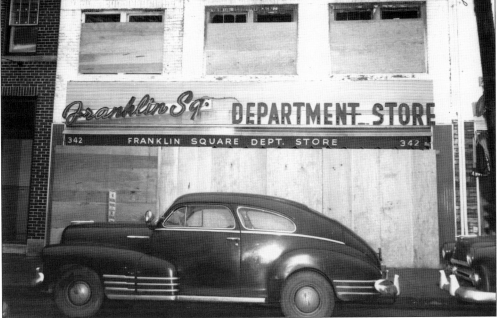

The Franklin Square Department Store was located at 342 Hempstead Turnpike (the numbers have been changed since), between Franklin Street and New Hyde Park Road. On February 15, 1956, the store and the apartments above it were destroyed by fire. This photograph shows the boarded-up store on the following day.

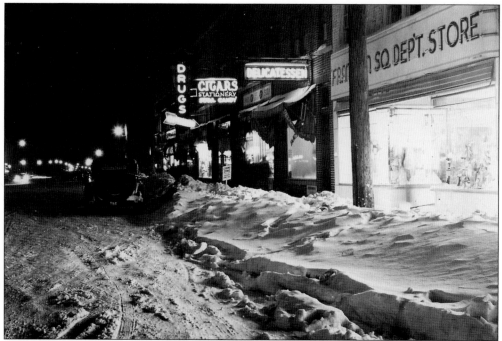

This nighttime winter scene shows Hempstead Turnpike in the early 1940s. The view is looking west, centering on the block between Franklin Street and New Hyde Park Road. Note long-gone businesses such as the Franklin Square Department Store.

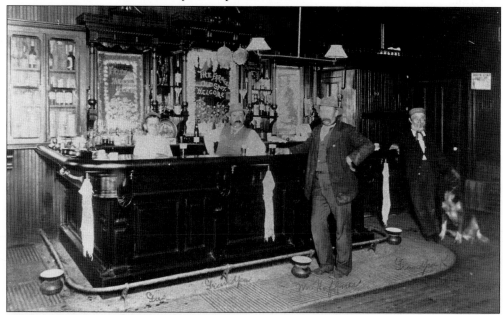

This is the saloon of the Kalb Hotel, known as the "Farmers Old Spot." The ornate bar was located in the middle of the hotel. In the picture are a boy named Gus, proprietor August Kalb, and patrons Mr. Hoeffner and Grandpa Kreischer. Note the lettering on the mirrors and the gas lamps over the bar—there was no electricity in Franklin Square when this picture was taken around 1910.

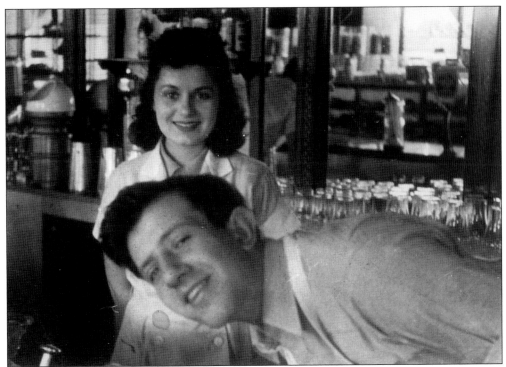

One of the leading businesses in Franklin Square from the 1930s until the early 1960s was Manos' Ice Cream Parlor. The business was located in the Hoffman block at the east corner of Hempstead Turnpike and New Hyde Park Road. In this photograph from the late 1930s, Doris Manos and her brother Peter stand behind the counter of their ice cream parlor.

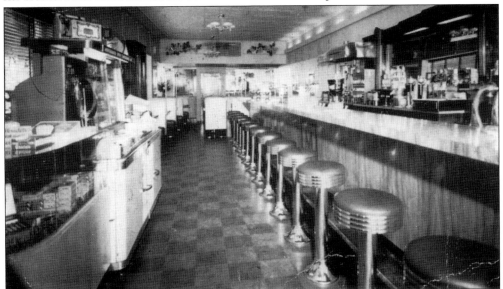

This photograph, originally produced as a postcard, shows the interior of Manos' Ice Cream Parlor around 1938. Note the fountain and counter at right. To the rear and left were booths. The cash register is at front left. Manos' was well known for its homemade ice cream. The menu also included soda, luncheon items, and the like. Candy and cigars were also sold in the showcase at left.

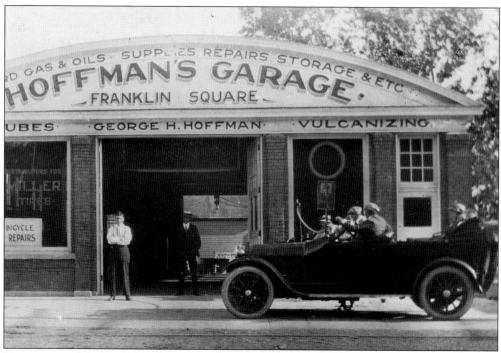

This picture of the Hoffman Garage on Hempstead Turnpike dates from 1917. The building was later modernized into the Hoffman Chevrolet showroom. In the late 1950s, the building was transformed into Astoria Federal Savings Bank. At one time, Hoffman's was the only gas station between Hempstead and the city line.

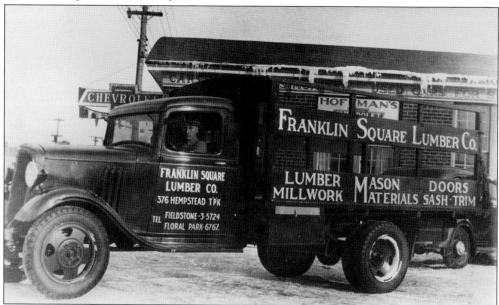

William Hoffman, proprietor of the Franklin Square Lumber Company, is pictured in the driver's seat of the company truck in this photograph from around 1939. The picture, looking east, was taken at Hoffman's Service Station (owned by Hoffman's brother August) on the east corner of Franklin Avenue and Hempstead Turnpike.

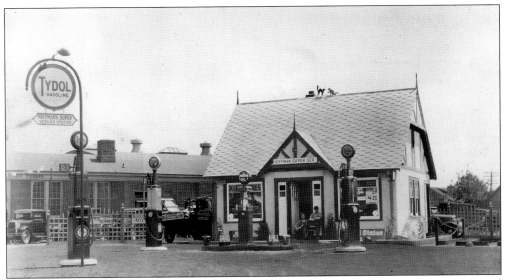

In 1929, the Hoffman Hotel, located at the east corner of Franklin Avenue and Hempstead Turnpike, was destroyed by fire. Shortly thereafter, August Hoffman built Hoffman's Super Service Station on the site. The station was once the busiest in Nassau County. This view was taken shortly after the service station was completed in 1929 or 1930. The Hoffman Chevrolet building is at left.

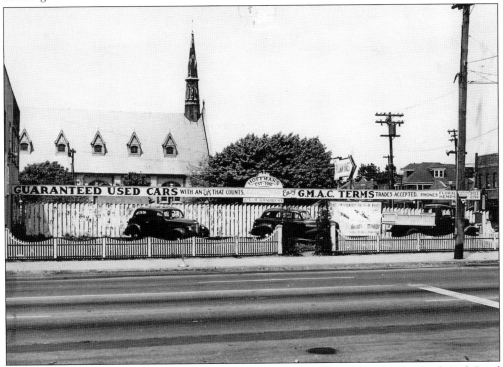

The Hoffman used car lot at the northwest corner of Hempstead Turnpike and New Hyde Park Road is the subject of this photograph dating from 1938. The Hoffman Chevrolet firm was founded by George Hoffman in 1916. Its main building was located on the south side of Hempstead Turnpike at the present site of Astoria Federal Savings from 1916 until the 1950s.

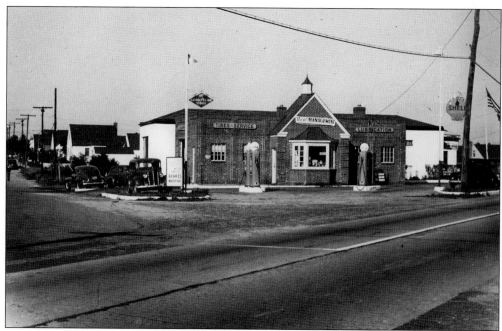

This photograph shows the intersection of Franklin Avenue (right) and Scherer Boulevard (left) as it appeared around 1941. The Shell gas station still stands in 2011, though it has been converted to other retail uses. Note the narrow concrete paving of Franklin Avenue, which was a two-lane road in those days. In spite of the changes, the view is still recognizable over 60 years later.

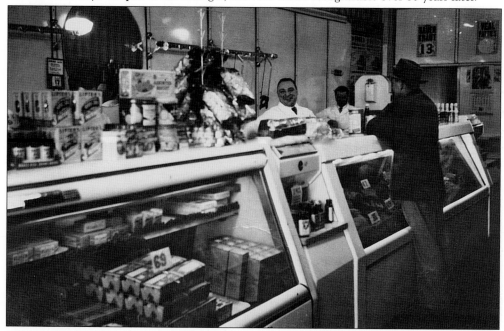

Koenig's Butcher Shop, located on Hempstead Turnpike near Grange Street, was a popular local business for decades. Here, Richard Koenig (left) is shown behind the counter of his business in the early 1950s. Franklin Square's business district has traditionally consisted of small businesses such as Koenig's Market. (Courtesy of Christine Smith.)

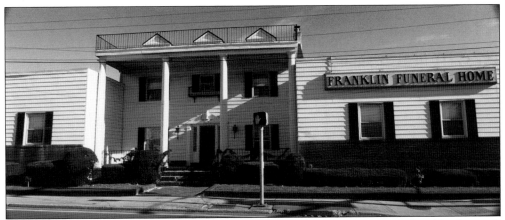

The Franklin Funeral Home was built in 1923 by Andrew Hoffman, owner of a local lumberyard, as a home for his family. Andrew and his wife, Mary, raised four children there. In 1939, Thomas Dalton bought the property and it became a funeral home. In 1957, Joseph Ongaro bought it, and in 1961, the Franklin Funeral Home opened in its current location. The home was renovated and expanded in 1978.

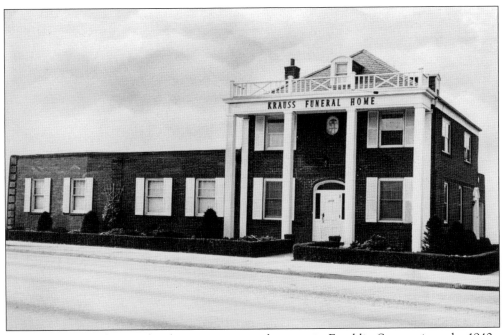

The Krauss Funeral Home has been a prominent business in Franklin Square since the 1940s. The firm was founded in Elmont in the early 1900s by Charles Krauss. In June 1952, the business was sold to the Christensen family. This view of the Krauss Funeral Home, at the east corner of Hempstead Turnpike and Scherer Boulevard, dates from July 1953.

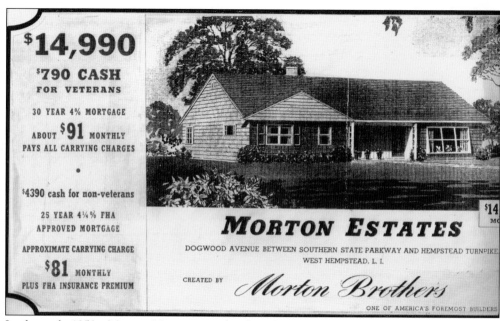

$14,990

$790 CASH
FOR VETERANS

30 YEAR 4% MORTGAGE
ABOUT $91 MONTHLY
PAYS ALL CARRYING CHARGES

•

$4390 cash for non-veterans

25 YEAR 4¼% FHA
APPROVED MORTGAGE

APPROXIMATE CARRYING CHARGE
$81 MONTHLY
PLUS FHA INSURANCE PREMIUM

MORTON ESTATES

DOGWOOD AVENUE BETWEEN SOUTHERN STATE PARKWAY AND HEMPSTEAD TURNPIKE
WEST HEMPSTEAD, L. I.

CREATED BY *Morton Brothers*

ONE OF AMERICA'S FOREMOST BUILDERS

In the early 1950s, Morton Homes were developed in the southern area of Franklin Square, west of Dogwood Avenue. The so-called "Morton ranches" proved to be very popular. Several hundred were built on gently curving streets. As shown here, the cost was $14,990 with a monthly mortgage payment of $81. The development has always had a strong neighborhood spirit and boasts its own civic association.

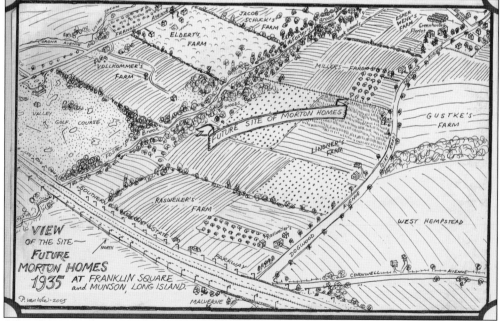

The future site of Morton Homes as it would have appeared in 1935 is depicted in this drawing. Note Dogwood Avenue, in those days a dusty farm road, and Foster's Brook, with its wooded banks. At the bottom is Southern State Parkway and at the far left is the Valley Golf Course fronting on Franklin Avenue.

46

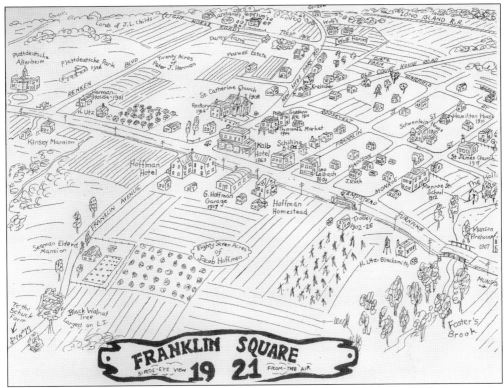

This bird's-eye view of central Franklin Square gives a general, if simplified, idea of the community as it existed in 1921. At that time, most of the community was clustered around Kalb's Hotel and St. Catherine of Sienna Church, north of Hempstead Turnpike. The major residential streets were Franklin Street, Madison Avenue, Monroe Street, Garfield Street, and Roosevelt Street, along with New Hyde Park Road and Hempstead Turnpike.

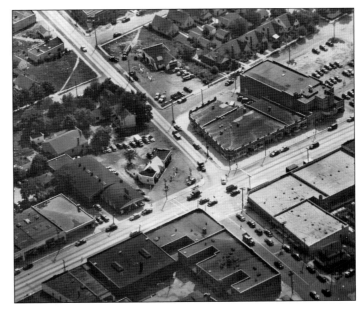

This aerial photograph of downtown Franklin Square dates from 1949. Pictured is the very center of the business district at the major intersection of Hempstead Turnpike and New Hyde Park Road. Franklin Avenue is at the upper right center of the photograph. The Franklin National Bank building (extreme left) and the curving roof of Hoffman Chevrolet are visible, and August Hoffman's gas station is next to Hoffman Chevrolet. Note the large Franklin Theater building at far right center.

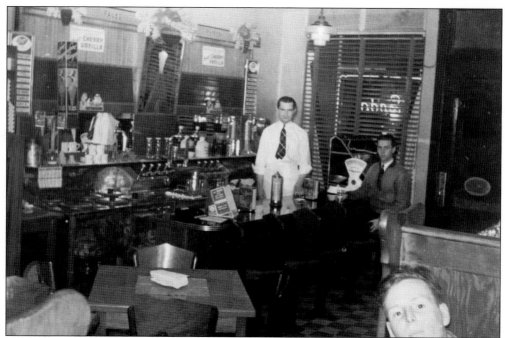

For many years (1930s to 1950s), there was an ice cream parlor next to the Franklin Theater on Hempstead Turnpike. This mid-1930s photograph was taken inside the ice cream parlor, which was owned by Edward Cornwell (standing, behind counter). Kenneth Hults is sitting at the counter, and Bob Jones is in the foreground.

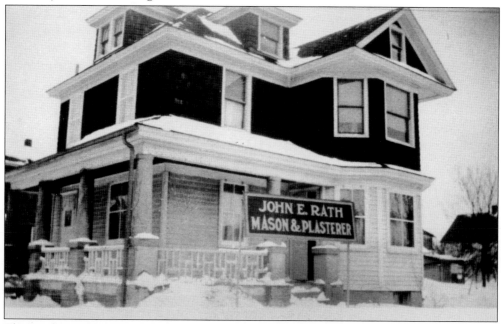

This is a late-1920s view of the John E. Rath house, located on the east side of Madison Street just off Hempstead Turnpike. This old home was built around 1912 and is no longer standing. Rath lived here for several decades but moved to Garden City South in the 1950s. The house was torn down in the early 1970s to make way for new single-family homes.

Three

An Active Community

In the early 20th century, Franklin Square was a small community of several hundred people. Longtime residents remember that in those days "everyone knew everyone else by name." Neighbors worked together to accomplish community improvements. The Franklin Square Community League, founded in the mid-1920s, lobbied for improved post office facilities and home delivery of mail. To facilitate these improvements, volunteers assigned house numbers to local homes and raised money for metal street signs. The league also sponsored Memorial Day and Fourth of July observances. Beginning in 1907, local farmers organized two local fire departments, which were unified into the Franklin Square and Munson Fire Department in 1924. The members raised money and built the firehouses themselves while protecting both life and property. The Franklin Square Public Library began similarly when volunteers went door to door asking for books and donations. Community volunteers originally staffed the first library, which was located in the basement of the Monroe Street School.

The variety of organizations in Franklin Square—then and now—reflects an active community. Through the years, the spirit of volunteerism has improved and shaped the community. Although Franklin Square now counts nearly 30,000 residents, the close-knit community life helps preserve a small-town ambience.

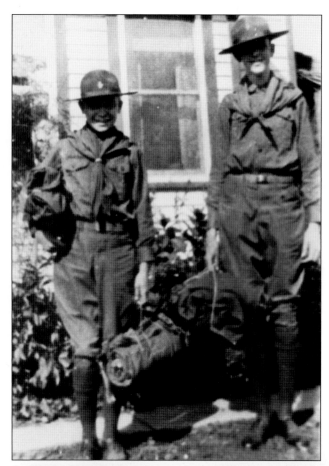

Two of the very first Franklin Square Boy Scouts, Harold Greene (left) and Harrison Quinn, both members of Troop No. 93, are shown in this photograph from October 12, 1942. The boys are about to depart on a Scout trip. They are standing next to the Quinn home at 114 Monroe Street.

This photograph depicts Franklin Square's original Boy Scout Troop, Troop No. 93. Here, the boys participate in the village's Fourth of July celebration in 1925. The scout leader is at left. In the early days of the troop, the boys did not have to go far to do wilderness camping; they walked to Wood's Pond off Nassau Boulevard and spent the weekend there.

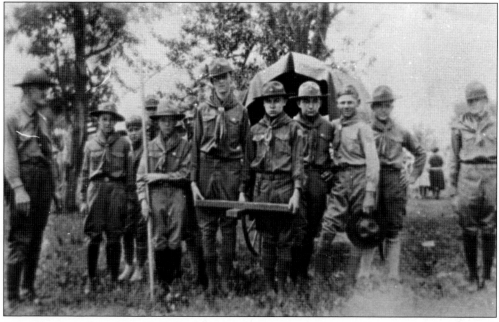

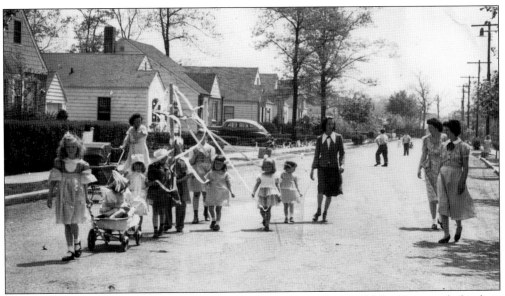

On May 1, 1948, a group of Franklin Square mothers organized a small May Day parade for their children. In this photograph, the group makes its way north on Fendale Street, just south of Naple Avenue. At the end of the street was Wenk's farm. Note traditional maypole carried by the children and the large oak trees among the houses constructed less than 10 years earlier.

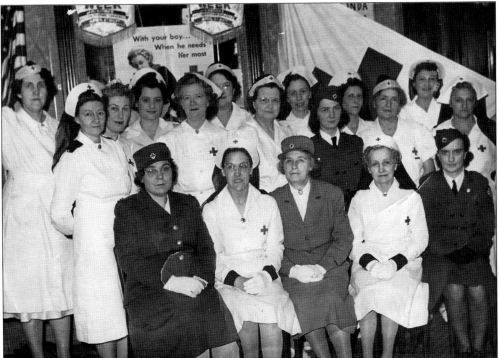

This 1942 picture of the Franklin Square Red Cross Organization illustrates one way that Franklin Square helped support the war effort—the community formed their own chapter of the Red Cross to assist in medical relief work. They raised money and served as nurses. This photograph was taken at a Red Cross benefit.

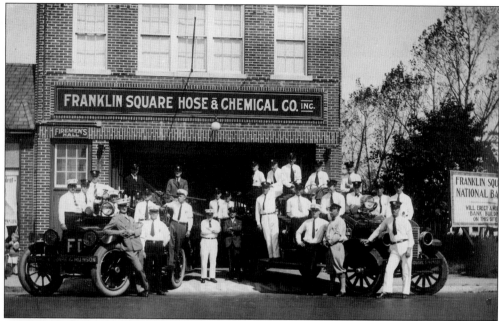

This photograph, from September 23, 1928, shows the old Franklin Square Hose and Chemical Company firehouse, built in 1926. The firehouse was located on Hempstead Turnpike between Madison and Franklin Streets. A siren can be seen on top of the house, and the meeting hall was upstairs.

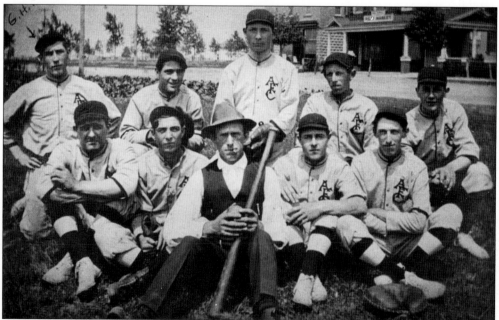

This photograph of the Franklin Athletic Club Baseball Team was taken shortly after the team's organization in March 1915. George Hoffman is in the second row at far left, and the Schuck boys are also in the second row. The team played semipro baseball and won the Long Island Championship in 1925. The manager at center is believed to be Samuel Schroeter. Behind the team is New Hyde Park Road, just south of St. Catherine of Sienna Church.

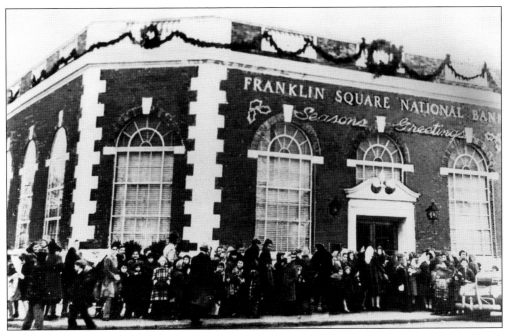

As part of a creative public relations campaign, the Franklin Square National Bank held popular Christmas shows for children in the 1940s. The shows were held on the banking floor and usually consisted of a puppet show and an appearance by Santa Claus. In this 1943 photograph, parents and children line up in anticipation of an afternoon show.

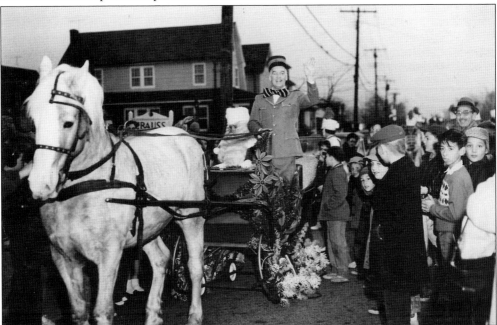

In the late 1940s, broadcast personality Ray Heatherton (known as the Merry Mailman) came to Franklin Square as part of a Christmas promotion. Here, Heatherton is escorted by Santa Claus, complete with sleigh. The photograph was taken at the corner of Scherer Boulevard and Hempstead Turnpike. A sign for Krauss Funeral Home is partially visible behind the horse.

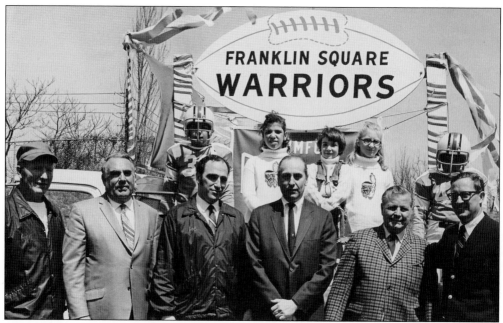

This photograph was taken in April 1970 at the opening day parade and ceremonies of the Garden City South Little League, held at the Cherry Valley Field on Cherry Valley Avenue. Included in the picture are, from left to right, Ray Miller, Franklin Square Warriors; Francis T. Purcell, Hempstead Town presiding supervisor; unidentified; Joseph P. van Wie, president, Garden City South Little League; Assemblyman Marigiotta; Congressman John Wydler.

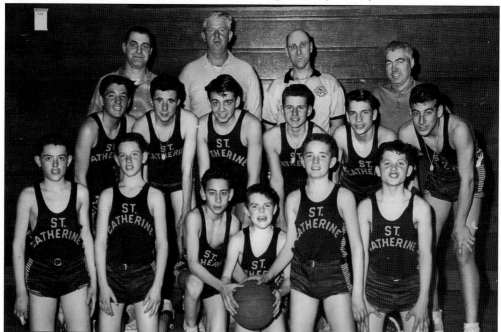

The St. Catherine of Sienna Church CYO (Catholic Youth Organization) basketball team posed for this team picture in 1958. In the 1950s and 1960s, St. Catherine's had quite an active CYO that specialized in basketball. Practice was generally held in the Carey High School gym.

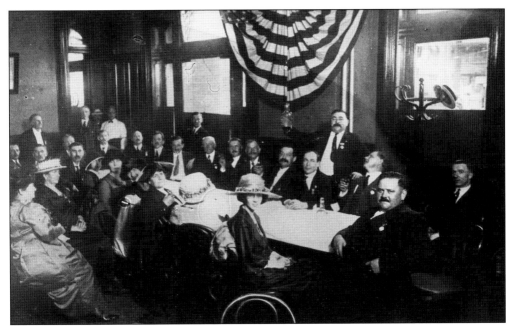

This c. 1917 photograph shows a typical meeting of the Hempstead Liederkranz, a singing society made up of Franklin Square German Americans. The meeting took place in the Kalb Hotel dining room, for the Liederkranz always met in Franklin Square. In the foreground is Max Thomala, a local butcher who founded the Liederkranz. Thomala, an immigrant from Breslau, Germany, served as president of the organization for 25 years.

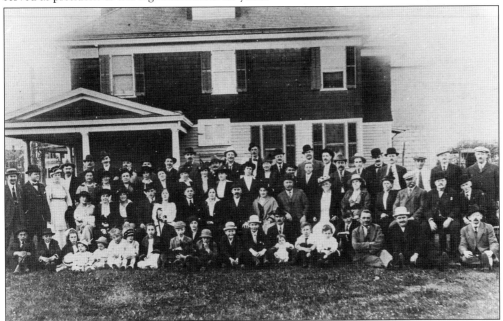

The Hempstead Liederkranz's annual picnic was held on September 17, 1916. Each year, the club sponsored a picnic that began the fall social season. This photograph was taken just north of the Kalb Hotel, on New Hyde Park Road in front of the old Thomala Meat Market. In the background is the side of the meat market, including the service porch and the ice hatch.

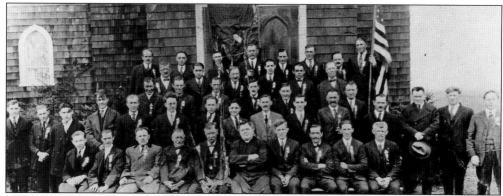

The Holy Name Society of St. Catherine of Sienna Church is pictured here in 1923. In the center is Fr. Conrad B. Lutz. The photograph was taken on the steps of the original church. Note the Holy Name badges the men are wearing. Some of the old families represented in this picture include Schilling, Laibach, Kreischer, Hoffman, Kalb, and Schuck.

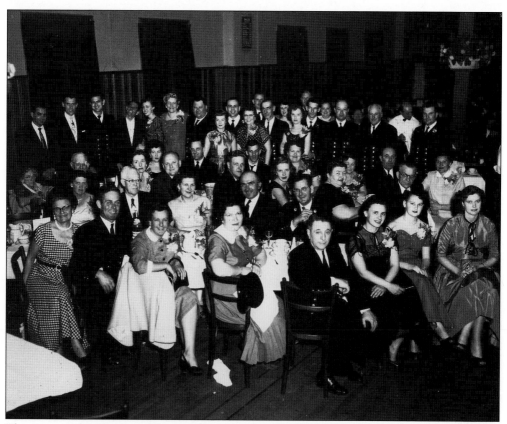

This is a social gathering of the Franklin Square and Munson Fire Department, held on April 16, 1955. The members of the fire department traditionally hold several social events each year, including an annual installation. In the mid-1900s, many of these events were held at the Plattdeutsche Park Restaurant.

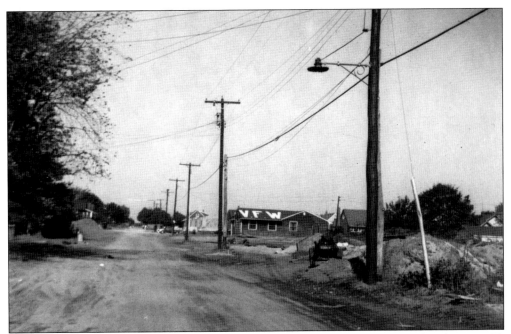

This view shows Lincoln Road as it appeared around 1951. The road was unpaved at this time. To the left is the future site of the Franklin Square Library, to the right is a filled creek bed—now the site of a parking lot. In the background, the roof sign of VFW Post 2718 is visible. Behind it are houses under construction.

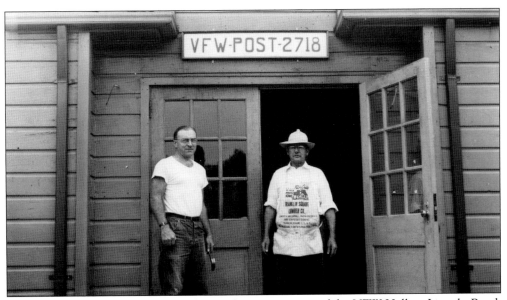

This c. 1952 photograph was taken during the construction of the VFW Hall on Lincoln Road. The original building, assembled in 1950 through 1952, consisted of two army surplus structures renovated by the VFW members themselves. In this photograph, two post members, tools in hand, take a break from work in front of the main door of the hall.

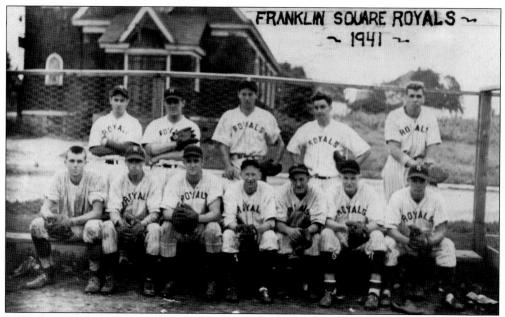

This photograph of the Franklin Square Royals baseball team in 1941 was taken at the team's baseball diamond, the present site of the St. Catherine of Sienna School. The players are, from left to right, (first row) Bruce Gehrke, Ken Hults, Mike Grobeck, George Von Essen, Joe Nicholson, Jack Vogt, and Eddie Regnell; (second row) Fred Herrmann, Ernie Kress, Buddy Weiner, Bucky Brenner, and Dave Bloodgood.

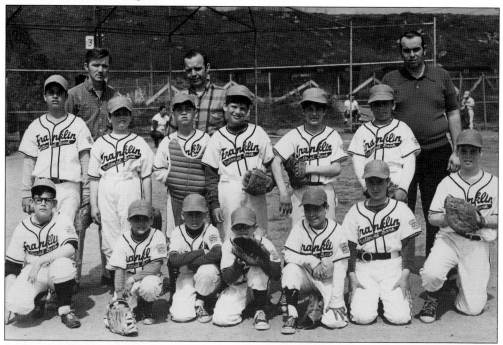

In this c. 1965 photograph, a Franklin Square Little League team poses for a tournament picture. The photograph was taken at a field in a neighboring town. Since the 1960s, most of the Franklin Square Little League games have been played at the Rath Park field.

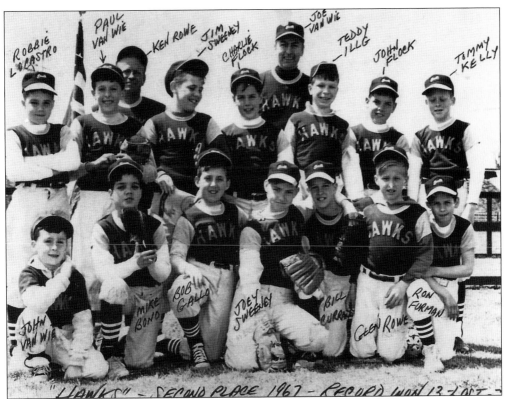

The Hawks, a minor-league team of the Garden City South Little League, posed for a team picture at the Cherry Valley Field on opening day in April 1967. Team members included, from left to right, (first row) John van Wie (batboy), Michael Bona, Robert Gallo, Joey Sweeney, ? Curran, Glen Rowe, and Ron Furman; (second row) Robert LoCastro, Paul van Wie, Coach Ken Rowe, Jimmy Sweeney, Charlie Flock, Teddy Illg, John Flock, and Tommy Kelly; (third row) coach Ken Rowe and manager Joseph van Wie.

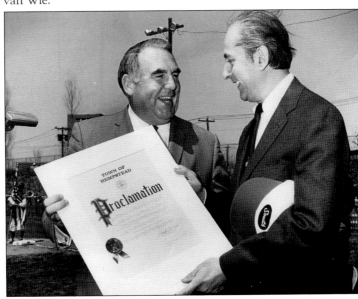

This photograph was taken at the opening day ceremonies of the Garden City South Little League in April 1970. Here, Hempstead Town presiding supervisor Francis T. Purcell presents a proclamation to league president Joseph P. van Wie. The picture was taken at the league's Cherry Valley Avenue field.

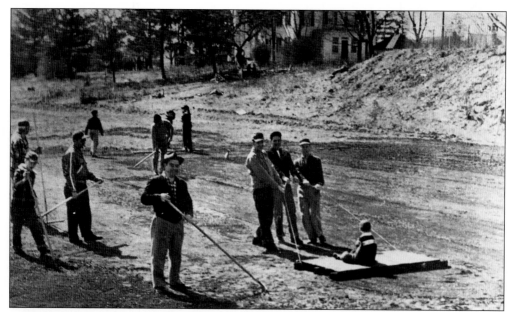

In 1955, the Garden City South Little League moved its field from the present site of Carey High School to the west corner of Cherry Valley Avenue and Hempstead Turnpike. This photograph was taken as a number of fathers and sons from the Little League were leveling and preparing the fields for play. In 1958, the league moved its field once again north to the present site on Cherry Valley Avenue.

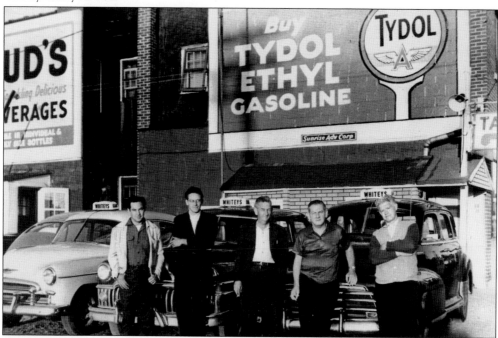

Whitey's Taxi was a long-established firm in Franklin Square. This photograph, which dates from the 1950s, shows the taxis and drivers at the taxi stand on Hempstead Turnpike, between New Hyde Park and Pacific Street. Behind them is the building that currently houses the Ramona-Lee Pastry Shop. The lot in the foreground is now a Taco Bell parking lot.

Rath Park was largely complete when this picture was taken on May 7, 1959. Here, John E. Rath (left) looks over park blueprints with Hempstead Town officials. The pool's diving board is in the background. Rath Park was so named after a variety of community groups petitioned the town to honor John E. Rath.

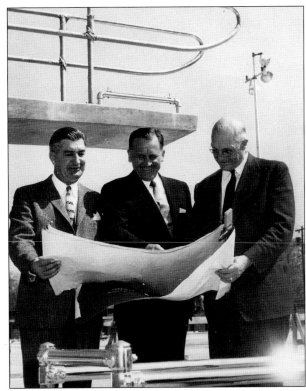

Much of central Franklin Square can be seen in this aerial view of Rath Park from June 1959. Hempstead Turnpike can be seen in the background. In the foreground is the Rath Park pool and parking lot. Behind the pool are the baseball diamonds. Fenworth Boulevard is between the pool and the baseball fields.

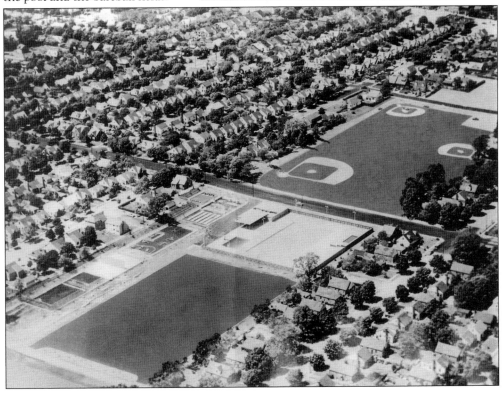

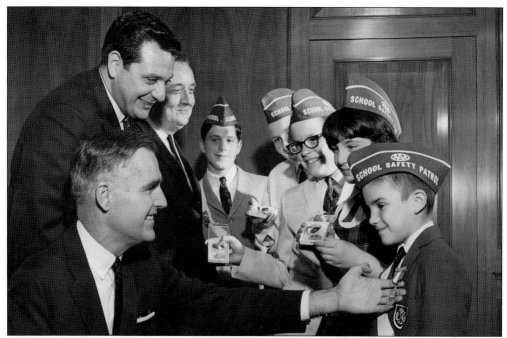

In this c. 1966 photograph, Nassau County executive Eugene Nickerson congratulates a group of Franklin Square School Safety Patrol members. The male students are believed to be award winners from the four Franklin Square public schools; the girl is from St. Catherine of Sienna School. The safety patrol encouraged students to walk home and cross streets in a safe manner.

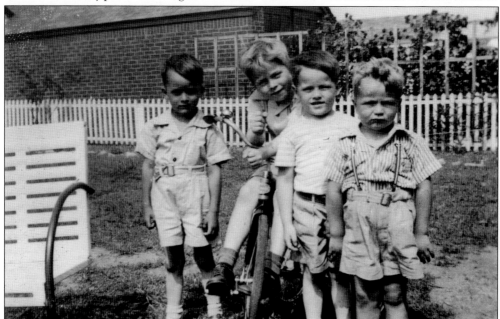

Thomas Martin (far right) is shown with some neighborhood friends in the backyard of his Rosegold Street home in this photograph from summer 1943. At the time this photograph was taken, many young families lived in this section of town, which was developed around 1940. The residents, many of whom had formerly lived in the city, enjoyed the suburban environment.

Rath Park was dedicated on June 6, 1959. To celebrate the new park and pool, a gala parade was held on Hempstead Turnpike with many bands and floats. This photograph depicts the Franklin Square Republican Club's float, featuring bathing beauties on lifeguard chairs and diving boards.

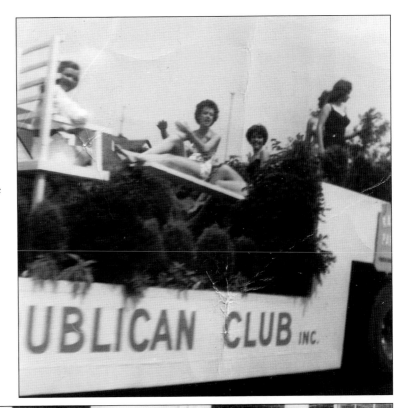

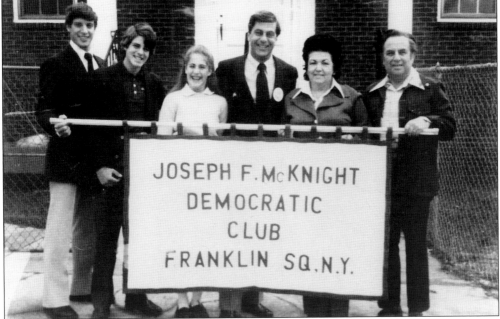

On Memorial Day in 1977, the Joseph F. McKnight Democratic Club (Franklin Square Democratic Club) joined the traditional parades in Franklin Square. Pictured in front of the American Legion Hall on Randolph Avenue (the assembly point) are, from left to right, Peirez's three children, county executive candidate David Peirez, Thelma Sardone, and Joseph Sardone.

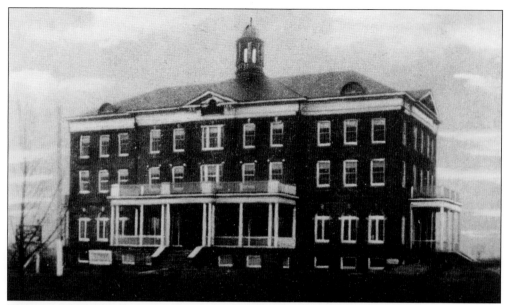

This view of the Plattdeutsche Altenheim (Old Folks Home) is derived from a picture postcard from around 1923. At that time, the Altenheim was a new building with about 50 residents. This photograph was taken looking north on Hempstead Turnpike. In the years since, additional apartments have been constructed in the rear of the building.

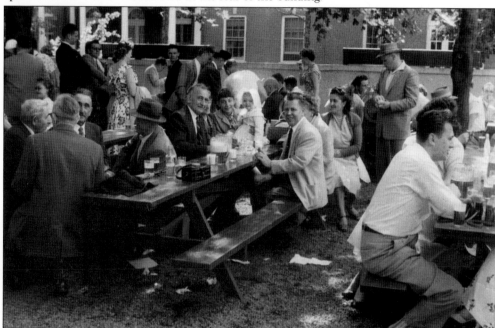

The Plattdeutsche Park Restaurant has been a center of German American life in the New York metropolitan area since 1916. In this photograph from the 1950s, a group of German Americans from the Gottschee region of Slovenia enjoys a summer afternoon. Included in the group are Matthias Gladitsch, Philip Schwender, Dorothy Weininger Doktor, Waltraud Gladitsch Tripoli, Joan Weininger Tramm, Marie Kosel Schwender, Resie Gladitsch Spalany, and Rosemary Spalany Bradshaw. (Courtesy of Rosemary Bradshaw.)

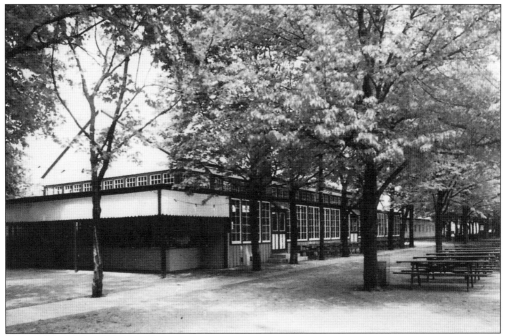

This view of the *biergarten*, or beer garden, of the Plattdeutsche Park dates from the 1960s. Plattdeutsche Park, a popular meeting place for German American clubs and cultural events, attracts people from throughout the New York area. The building at left is the headquarters of the Brooklyn Schuetzen Corps. The scene of this photograph is just west of Renken Boulevard.

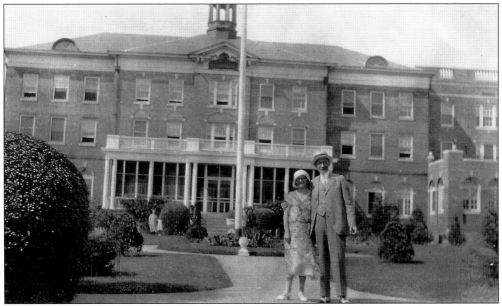

This c. 1933 photograph was taken in front of the Plattdeutsche Altenheim (Old Folks Home) on Hempstead Turnpike. The building, constructed in 1922, had been enlarged, with an east wing visible at extreme right in this photograph. At right is Martin Renken, then president of the Plattdeutsche Altenheim Gesellschaft. Renken served as president for nearly 25 years; he also headed the Renken Dairy system whose products were sold throughout the New York area.

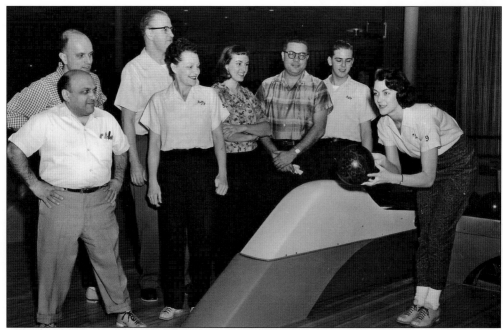

This photograph captures the Franklin National Bank bowling team in the 1950s. Activities such as this encouraged a sense of pride and cooperation in the bank. By the 1960s, the Franklin National Bank had emerged as one of the largest banks in the United States. The picture was taken at the Franklin Bowl on Franklin Avenue, which has since closed.

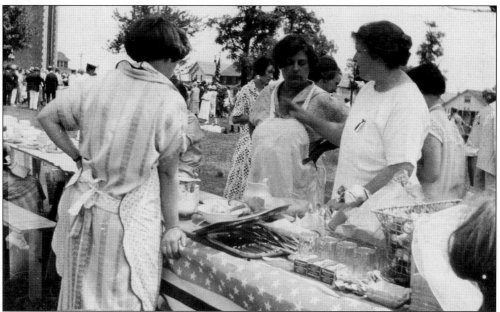

In 1925, Franklin Square's Fourth of July celebratory parade and reception were held at the Monroe Street School yard. This picture shows Carolyn Stringham (left, back to camera), Mrs. Garlic (left), and Ethel Quinn as they supervise the refreshment table. The field in which the festivities took place was located just south of Monroe Street School. The school itself is visible at far left in the picture.

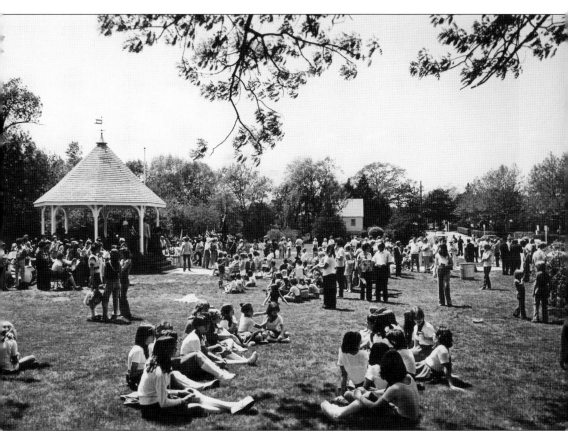

This Victorian gazebo was built by the Ben Franklin Bicentennial Committee as a lasting reminder of the 200th birthday of the United States of America. This is a general view of the crowd assembled for the gazebo dedication on May 21, 1978. Note the youth groups and other organizations filling this section of Rath Park. This westward view shows Naple Avenue at right.

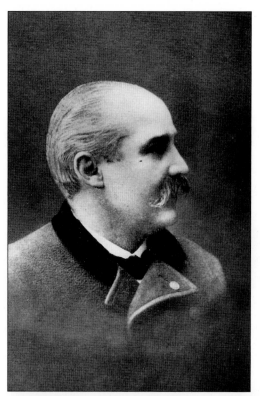

In 1901, Harry Munson of New York City purchased a farm in the area then known as Washington Square (now eastern Franklin Square and part of West Hempstead). Harry Munson was a businessman who served and was wounded in the Civil War. In honor of Harry Munson, the surrounding area was named for him. This photograph of Harry Munson dates from the early 20th century.

Pictured here in 1930 are the Franklin Square Hose and Chemical Co. trucks. At the wheels are Pete Blumke and Art Rasmussen. The old firehouse was located on Hempstead Turnpike between Madison Avenue and Franklin Street. The volume of traffic on Hempstead Turnpike and the need for a more modern facility resulted in the construction of the present-day firehouse on Liberty Place.

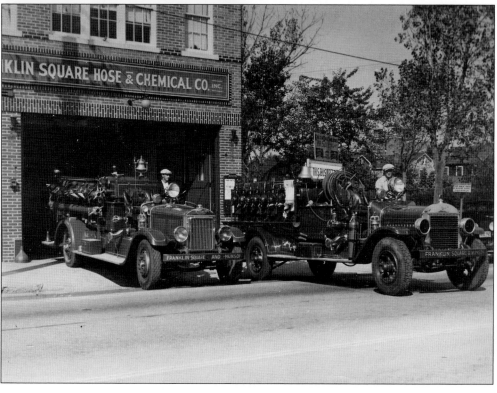

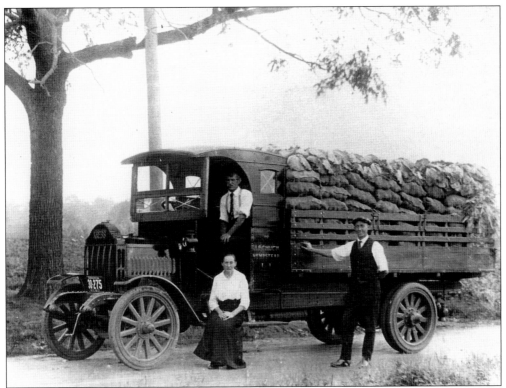

This 1917 image shows the Schuck farm truck on Franklin Avenue, looking east near the present site of Ascension Lutheran Church. At left is a landmark black walnut tree, one of the largest of its kind in those days. Mr. and Mrs. Schuck are shown sitting on the truck. The cargo includes cabbage, potatoes, and corn.

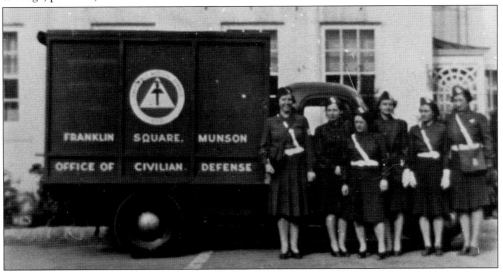

During World War II, the local Civilian Defense organization was an important part of the war effort. Here, a contingent of female members stands next to the organization's truck. This picture was taken in the rear parking lot of the Franklin Square National Bank building in the winter of 1944.

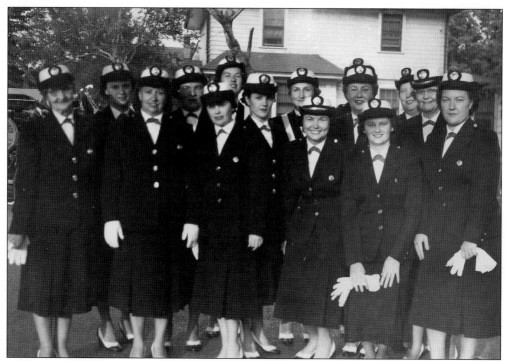

This is the Fire Department Ladies Auxiliary preparing for a parade on August 2, 1958. The parade was held at Fireman's Day, in the village of Floral Park. The group won a prize that day for "Best Appearance."

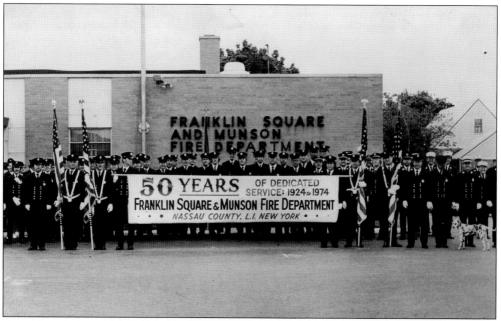

This is the official Golden Jubilee photograph of the Franklin Square and Munson Fire Department, taken in front of the firehouse on Liberty Place. In 1974, the department celebrated the anniversary with a gala parade and other festivities.

Four

SCHOOL LIFE

Because Franklin Square does not have its own village government, the local schools have always helped define the community. Franklin Square's first school, the Washington Square Common School, was located on Dogwood Avenue and Nassau Boulevard. Constructed in the early 19th century, it was originally a one-room facility. Walt Whitman, the famous American poet, served as a teacher in this school in 1840. Enlarged several times, the Washington Square School (also known as the Munson School House) closed in 1912 when separate school districts were created for Franklin Square and West Hempstead.

In 1912, a new, eight-room brick schoolhouse was constructed on Monroe Street in Franklin Square. Enlarged in 1926 to serve a growing population, Monroe Street School included grades one through eight. Local students first attended high school in Hempstead and, after 1930, attended Sewanhaka High School. Further population growth necessitated the construction of John Street School in 1936, Polk Street School in 1942, and Washington Street School in 1948. In 1956, Franklin Square received its own high school, named after H. Frank Carey, an energetic board of education president.

In 1956, St. Catherine of Sienna School opened, giving local students the option of a Catholic education.

The old Monroe Street School closed in the 1970s and was torn down several years later. Its site is now occupied by single-family homes. Older Franklin Square residents fondly remember Monroe Street as the center of community life in the early 20th century.

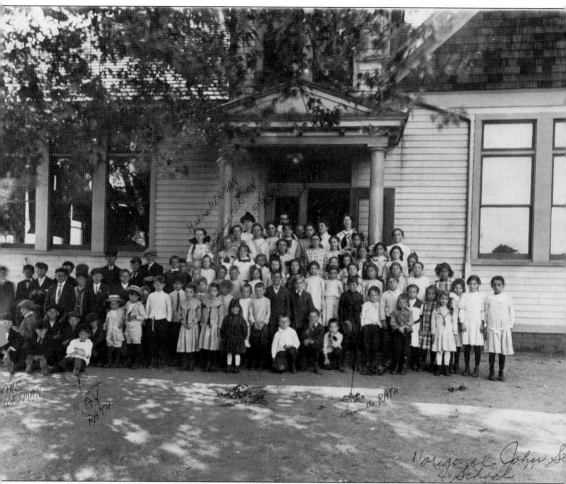

The Washington Square School was the original District 17 (Franklin Square) school and the forerunner of today's Franklin Square public schools. It was located at the fork of Nassau Boulevard (then called John Street) and Dogwood Avenue, hence the nickname "the Old John Street School." Washington Square School was constructed around 1840 as a one-room building; in the spring of that year, the famous poet Walt Whitman served as a teacher there. The Washington Square School closed in 1912 when West Hempstead was given its own district and a new brick schoolhouse was constructed in the middle of Franklin Square. This c. 1912 image shows the principal, Thomas LeRoy (center, top row), and other people, including Miss M. Lynch; Hans (John) Hoffman; Ray and Annette Rath (siblings of John Rath); and Hilda and Catherine Herman (daughters of school board member Peter J. Herman).

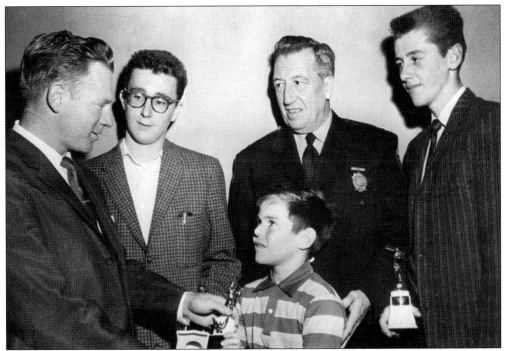

Major League Baseball player Whitey Ford was the special guest at the Franklin Square Police Boys Club Sports Night on November 19, 1958, at the Washington Street School. In the photograph, Ford presents a trophy to Daniel Imbrenda. Also pictured here are, from left to right, Senior Award winner Bill Hackett, Capt. Joseph Barr, and Intermediate Award winner Bud Knittel.

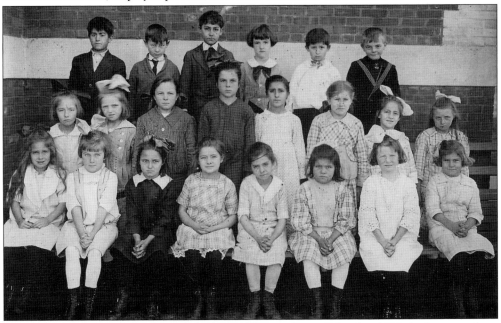

This photograph shows the third-grade class at Monroe Street School in 1916. At the time, there was only one class per grade, and Monroe Street was the only school in Franklin Square until 1936. In 1916, the population of Franklin Square was well under 1,000 people.

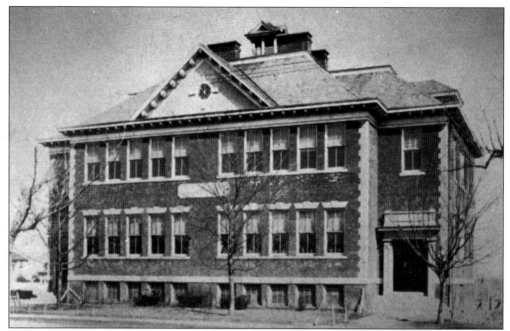

This photograph of Monroe Street School was taken in the winter of 1925–1926, shortly before the additions of more wings to the school. Monroe Street is in the foreground, and the view is looking east. This photograph appeared in advertisements for Franklin Square Gardens, a real estate development; prospective buyers were supposed to be impressed by the school facility.

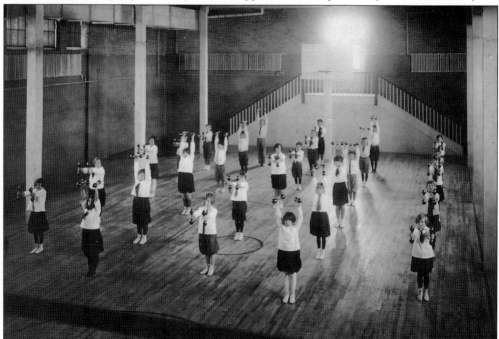

In 1926, Monroe Street School was expanded. The expansion program included the addition of a lunchroom and the installation of a gymnasium in the basement. This photograph of the gymnasium dates from the late 1920s. Here, a group of girls and boys exercise.

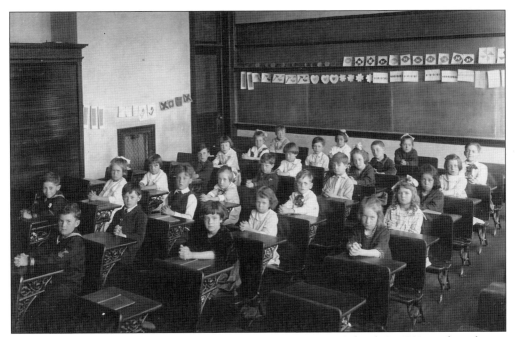

This 1921 picture shows a second-grade class at Monroe Street School. In 1921, students began school in the first grade. Kindergarten was added later. In the early 20th century, if a student wished to go to high school, they generally attended Hempstead High.

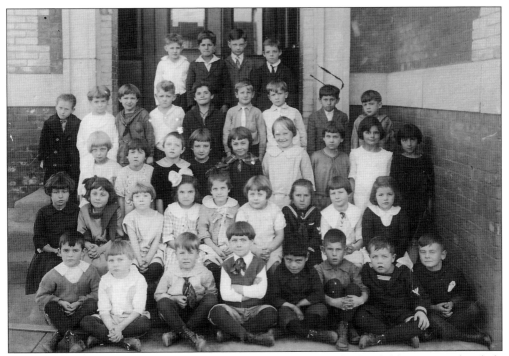

This is a 1923 first-grade class picture from Monroe Street School. The children pictured include Grace Kiefer, Christian Adams, Wilfred Hoffman, and Principal Thomas LeRoy's daughter, Molly Leroy.

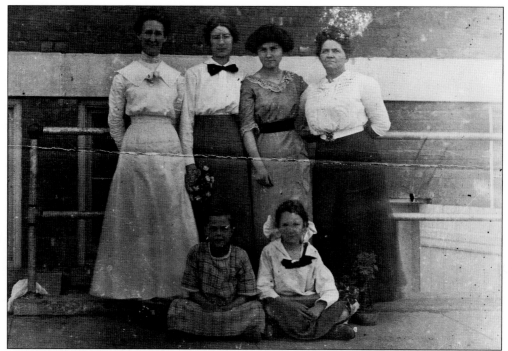

Four schoolteachers at Monroe Street School are pictured here around 1917. The teachers included Sara I. Bigelow, Miss Tallman, Miss Tuttle, and Elizabeth McMahon. The student seated at right is Dorothy McKenna. In the 1912–13 school year, Bigelow taught fifth and sixth grades; McMahon third and fourth; Mercie Ketcham first and second, and Mae A. Lynch first B grade. Principal Thomas LeRoy supervised the seventh and eighth grades.

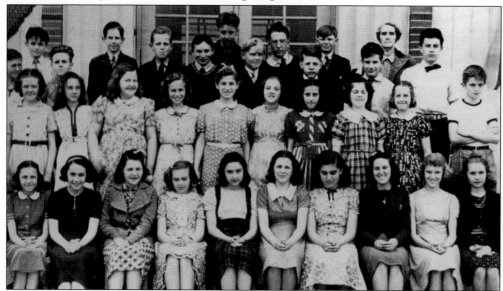

Pictured is a sixth-grade class at John Street School in 1939. The building was completed in 1936, and this was one of the original classes. The John Street School was constructed as part of the Works Progress Administration (WPA), one of thousands of public works projects designed to move the United States out of the Great Depression.

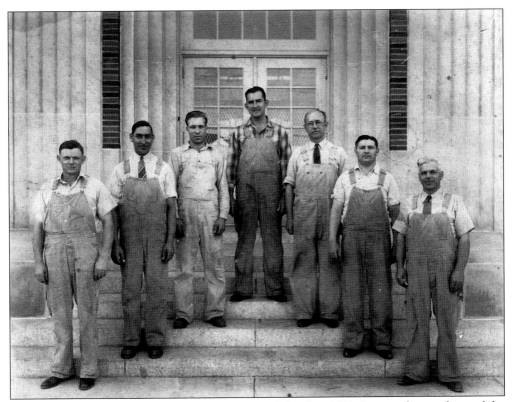

This picture shows the custodians of John Street School in 1941. It was taken in front of the school. Some of the Art Deco stone details of the school are visible in the background. The angular architectural lines of the school exemplify this style, which was prevalent in the 1920s and 1930s.

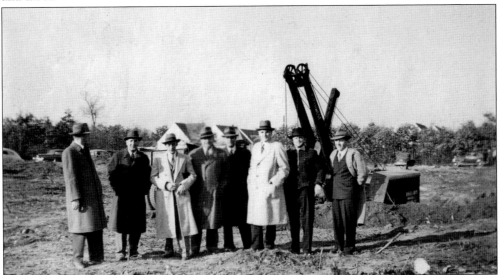

This photograph shows the board of education, plus several other citizens, at the ground breaking of Polk Street School on November 21, 1941. Included in the picture are H. Frank Carey, John Doyle, and James L. Wheelin.

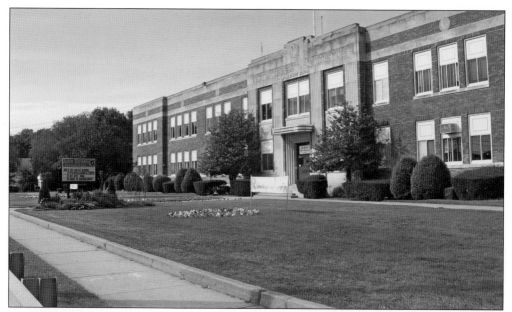

Until 1936, Monroe Street School was the only school in Franklin Square. In that year, John Street School was completed at a cost of $280,000. The Art Deco–style building was partially funded by Franklin D. Roosevelt's WPA. John Street School has been expanded twice in the last 60 years.

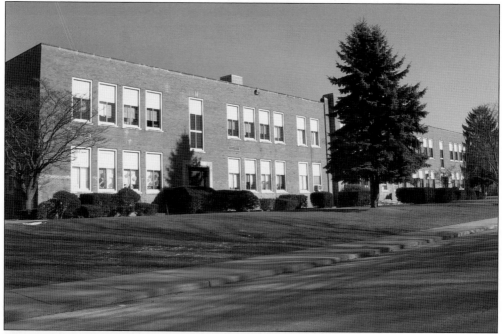

Because of rapid suburban development, Polk Street School was constructed to serve the students of southern Franklin Square in 1941 and 1942. Ground for the school was broken on November 21, 1941, just two weeks before the start of World War II. Had the board of education waited any longer, construction would have been delayed until 1947 due to the prohibition of civilian construction in wartime.

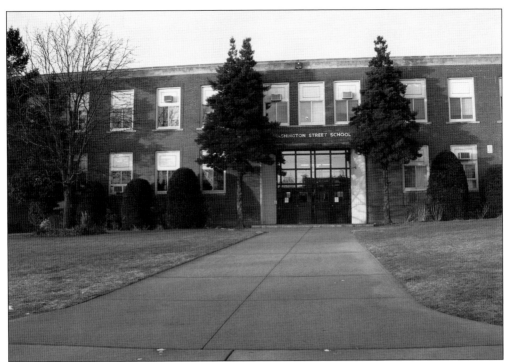

Franklin Square's fourth elementary school, Washington Street School, was constructed in 1948–1949. Somewhat larger than the other schools, Washington Street was used as a junior high school until H. Frank Carey High School opened in 1956. Washington Street School houses the offices of the Franklin Square School District. The Washington Street campus once included the land now occupied by Carey High School.

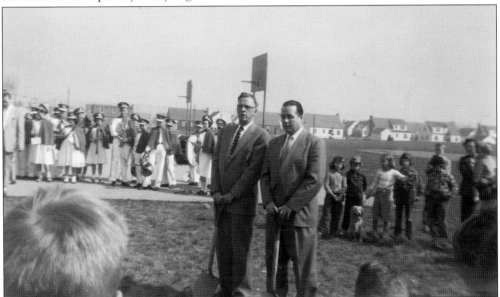

This picture commemorates the official ground breaking for H. Frank Carey High School, located on Poppy Avenue. At left is H. Frank Carey himself and on the right is Victor Kane, the Sewanhaka Board of Education president when this picture was taken in April 1955.

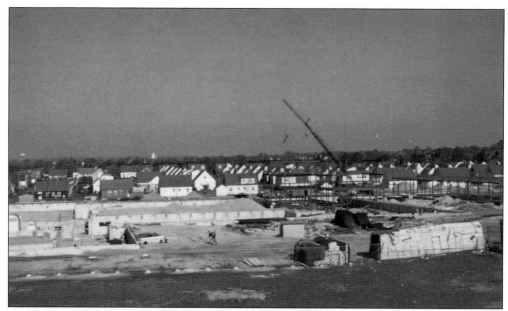

This October 1955 image is of H. Frank Carey High School under construction. Pictured is the foundation of Carey High School. This view, taken from the roof of Washington Street School, looks north toward Floral Park Road. Note the housing development in the background. Carey opened for classes in September 1956, even though construction was not yet complete.

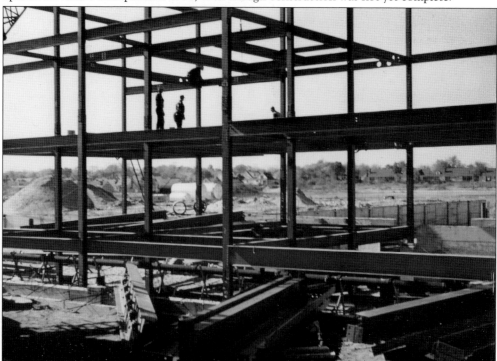

Franklin Square's H. Frank Carey High School was nothing but a skeleton when this photograph was taken in October 1955. Here is a typical construction scene, complete with workmen. The view is looking southwest. H. Frank Carey High School was completed in 1956.

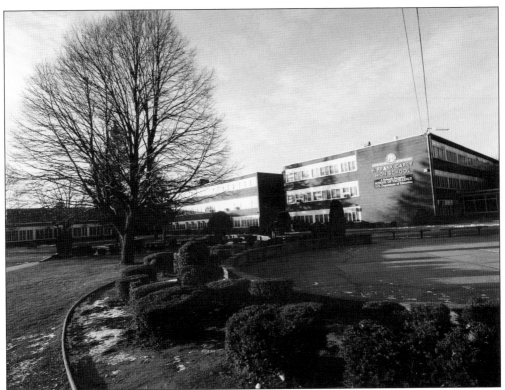

In the early 1900s, Franklin Square students enrolled at Hempstead High School if they wished to pursue their education beyond the eighth grade. In 1929, Franklin Square joined with neighboring districts to build Sewanhaka High School. Franklin Square students attended Sewanhaka in Floral Park until 1956 when H. Frank Carey High School opened. This photograph of Carey High was taken from a point near the northern end of Goldenrod Avenue.

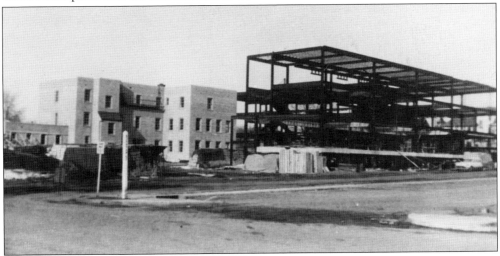

Pictured is St. Catherine of Sienna School under construction. This view, looking east from the corner of Holzheimer and Pacific Streets, was taken on March 26, 1956. The convent, nearing completion, is at left. The construction of St. Catherine's was the result of fundraising that began in the 1930s and a major fund drive launched in 1953.

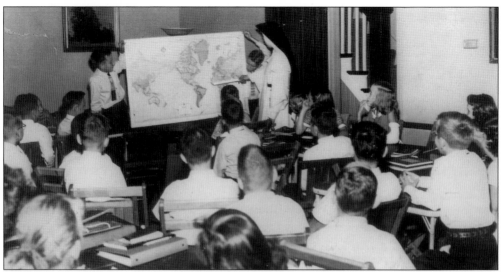

Ground was broken for St. Catherine of Sienna School on July 19, 1955, with classes scheduled for September 1956. Due to a steel strike, however, construction was delayed and the school was not ready in September. The parish decided that school would open anyway and improvised quarters were secured. This photograph shows a class taking place in the Franklin Funeral Home, across New Hyde Park Road from St. Catherine's.

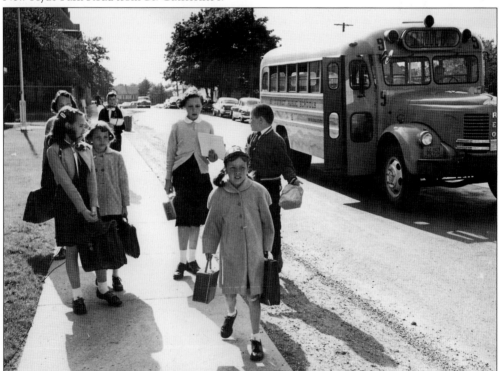

This picture of students outside St. Catherine of Sienna School probably dates from the fall of 1958, during the school's third academic year. The sidewalk, lawn, and shrubbery are still quite new in this photograph; curbing has not yet been installed. The view is from the west end of the school, looking east down Holzheimer Street toward New Hyde Park Road.

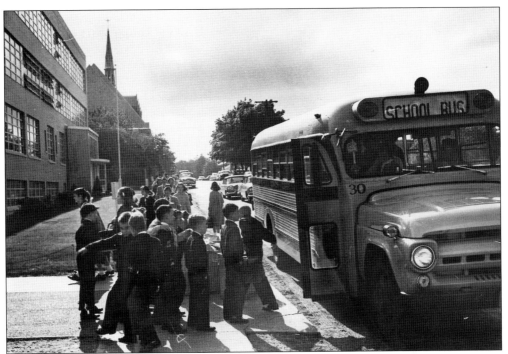

This photograph of students outside St. Catherine of Sienna School probably dates from fall 1958. The view is looking east on Holzheimer Street. At far left is the school building; behind it is the parish church. At this time, Holzheimer Street was still an uncurbed, dusty road.

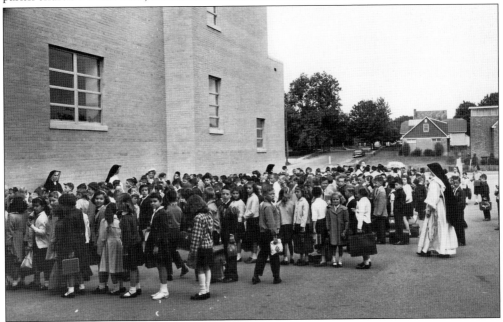

This is a view of St. Catherine of Sienna School yard in 1958. Here, the children line up at the beginning of the school day, supervised by several nuns. The view is from the portion of the school yard between the school and the convent. The Franklin Square Jewish Center is in the background at right; the street to the left of the Jewish Center is Lloyd Street (looking west).

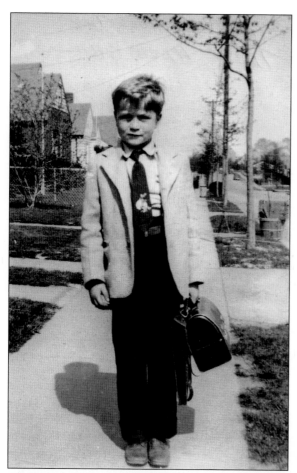

In May 1947, Thomas Martin of Rosegold Street posed for this picture outside his home as he was leaving for school. He was then in the second grade. The elementary schools of Franklin Square have traditionally played a central role in community life, and Thomas's walk to school has been repeated by many thousands of children over the years. The meaning of this photograph, then, can be understood by practically everyone.

Washington Street School was constructed on this land in 1948–1949. This is a general view of the school site, looking southeast from where the building now stands. The building stakes have already been laid out in preparation for excavation. The picture was taken on March 4, 1948. The homes closest to the building site are on Washington Street. The water tower at left is on Margaret Street.

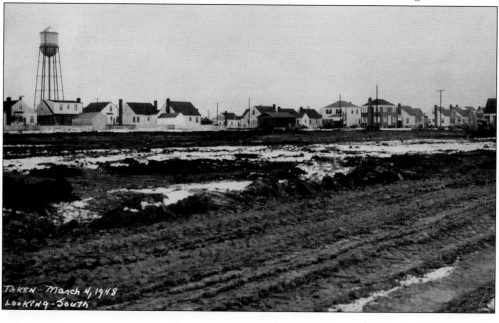

TAKEN - March 4, 1948
LOOKING - South

Five

ON THE MOVE

Franklin Square owes its existence as a community to a crossroad—the intersection of Hempstead Turnpike and New Hyde Park Road. It was at this site in the mid-19th century that Anton Staatz and Ludwig Schroeher both built small hotels to serve those who were "passing through." Hempstead Turnpike had been an important thoroughfare since colonial times, and in 1790, Pres. George Washington made his way down what was then a dirt road.

In the mid-20th century, it was said that Franklin Square was the largest town in America without a railway station. And since Franklin Square has never had a railroad, the people have always been dependent upon automobiles. The first automobile in town, a 1905 model, was owned by August Pfalzer, a farmer who lived on Hempstead Turnpike. Since then, the people of Franklin Square have shared the American love of the automobile. From an early date, the Hoffman Garage (and later the Hoffman Chevrolet dealership) was an important local hangout. The automobile, which provides both freedom and serious traffic to local residents, is a key element in Franklin Square life.

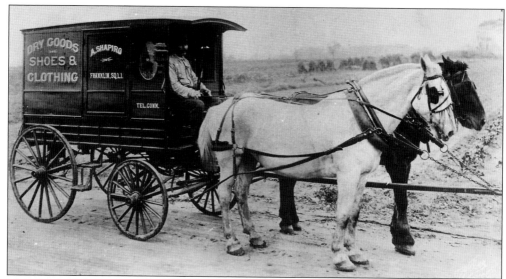

The Shapiro Dry Goods wagon is pictured here on New Hyde Park Road around 1915. This wagon enabled Shapiro to conduct business on the surrounding farmlands. His store was located just north of Washington Street. A. Shapiro holds the reins in his wagon, which was a welcome sight for many families, as it made it unnecessary to visit Hempstead for small purchases.

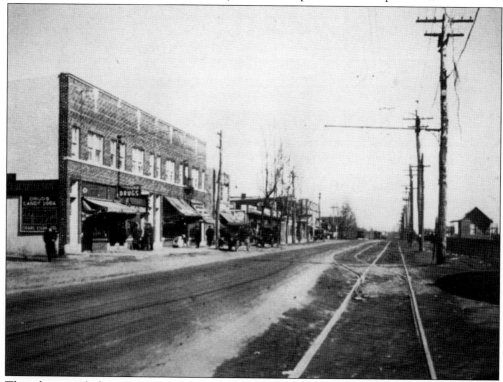

This photograph from 1924 or 1925 clearly shows Franklin Square's business district. In those years, the business district was only a block or two long. The photograph was taken at the east corner of Hempstead Turnpike and Franklin Avenue, looking east along Hempstead Turnpike. At extreme right is the Hoffman farm.

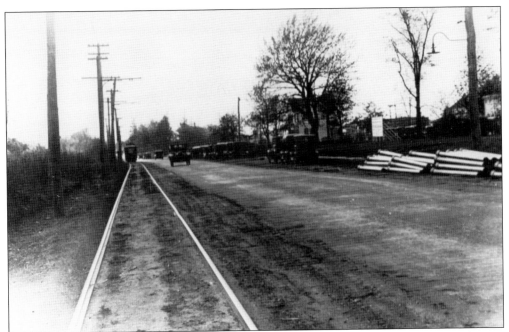

This 1922 photograph shows Hempstead Turnpike, looking west from Herman Boulevard. Note the trolley car and tracks. The construction materials for Plattdeutsche Altenheim (Old Folks Home) can be seen in the photograph at right. Much of the land along Hempstead Turnpike remained farmland into the 1940s.

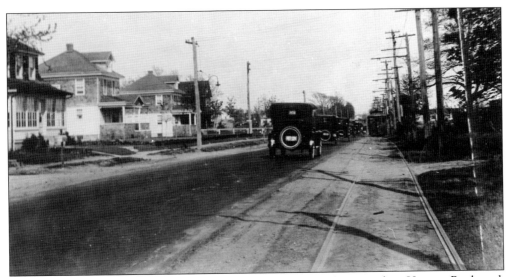

This 1922 photograph of Hempstead Turnpike shows the view looking east from Herman Boulevard. Note the trolley car, Sunday traffic, and the row of spacious homes at left. The center house was the home of Herman A. Utz, at the corner of today's Lexington Avenue. Hempstead Turnpike remained a toll road into the 1890s.

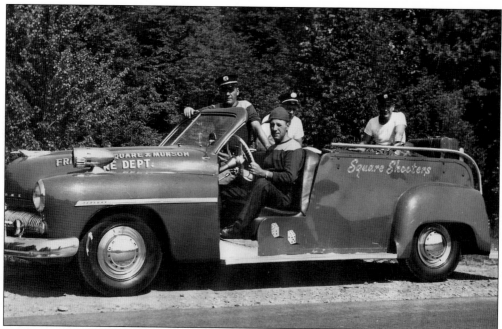

Members of the Franklin Square and Munson Fire Department tournament team gathered for this photograph around 1953. There have been a number of tournament teams over the years; at this time, the team was known as the "Square Shooters." Pictured is the tournament car. Note the dice, the symbol of the team.

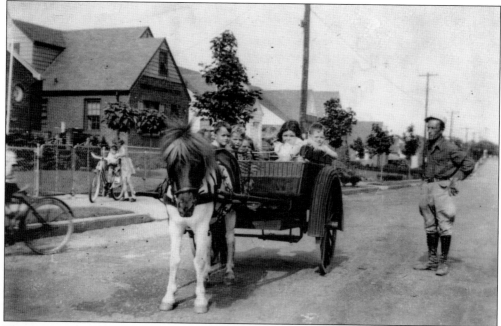

Thomas Martin and friends enjoy a pony cart ride near their Rosegold Street homes in this photograph from summer 1943. The driver charged a small amount of money for this thrilling opportunity, much loved by local children. In the 1940s, Franklin Square was still rural enough to boast horse pastures, one of which was located adjacent to today's Carey High School athletic field.

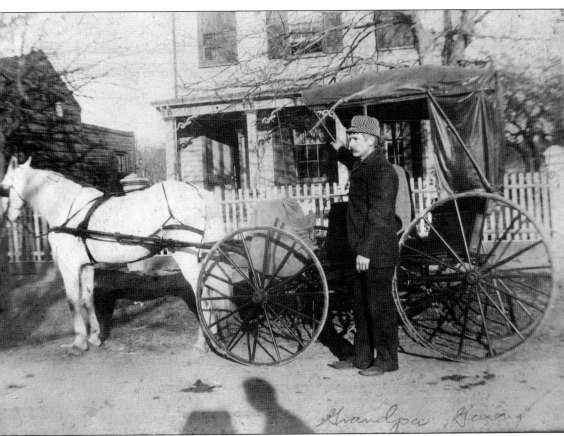

Grandpa Gaynor is pictured with his horse and buggy in front of his Court House Road home in this photograph from around 1910. The home was located near Garfield Street. The Gaynors settled in Franklin Square in the early 1900s and remained in the community for a century. The horse and buggy remained a common sight in Franklin Square until the 1920s. In the early 1900s, Franklin Square homes were generally located on Hempstead Turnpike, New Hyde Park Road, Court House Road, Franklin Avenue, Dogwood Avenue, or Tulip Avenue. There were no side streets in 1900. Few homes had electricity before 1917. The Gaynor home was a typical Franklin Square homestead of the time.

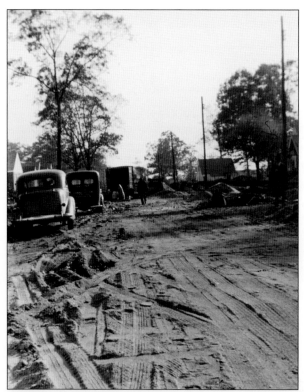

In the autumn of 1941, Ribbon Street in Franklin Square was still an unpaved road in the midst of a construction area. This 1941 photograph shows Ribbon Street, looking south toward Fenworth Boulevard from the middle of the Benris Avenue–Fenworth Boulevard block. This is an important photograph documenting a key aspect of Franklin Square's history—the building boom of 1936–1942.

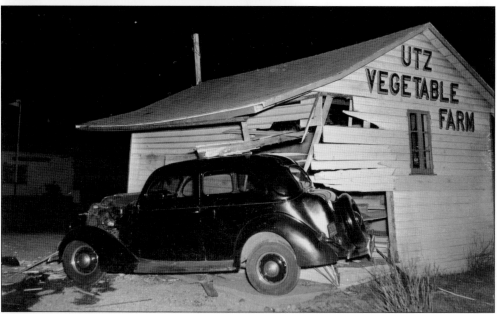

The Utz vegetable farm was operated by the son of blacksmith Herman Utz and was bound by Tulip Avenue, Renken Boulevard, the Plattdeutsche Park property, and the back lot line of houses on the east side of Barrymore Boulevard. Near the corner of Tulip Avenue and Renken Boulevard, the Utz family maintained a small wooden farm stand. In this 1941 photograph, the farm stand is shown in the aftermath of an automobile accident.

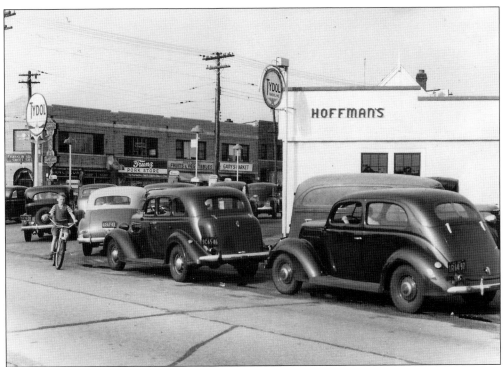

This unusual photograph depicts a gas line at Hoffman's gas station in the summer of 1942. World War II was in full swing at this time, and gas was a scarce, carefully rationed item. This is a side view of Hoffman's, with Franklin Avenue (then a narrow cement road) in the foreground. In the background is "Hoffman's Block" of stores on Hempstead Turnpike.

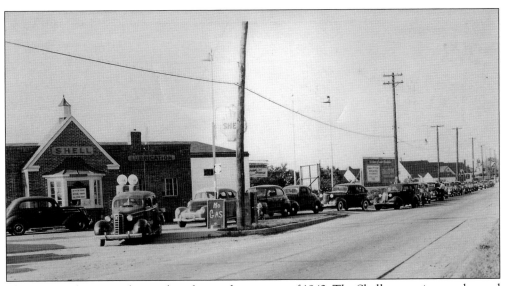

This picture shows another gas line during the summer of 1942. The Shell gas station was located at Franklin Avenue and Scherer Boulevard. A sign in the gas station window identifies the station as a rubber collection center (rubber was a scarce war material). Note the sign in front proclaiming "no gas."

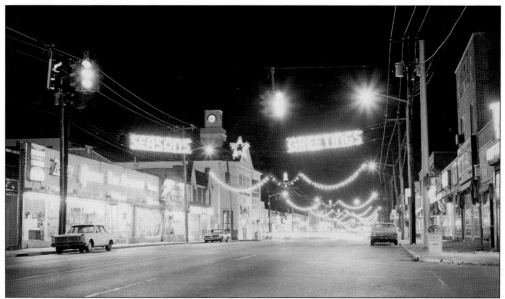

Franklin Square's annual lights display is the subject of this photograph taken around 1970. For many years in the 1960s and 1970s, Christmas lights were strung across Hempstead Turnpike in various designs. The display was sponsored by the Franklin Square Chamber of Commerce. This photograph was taken at the east corner of Madison Avenue and Hempstead Turnpike, looking west.

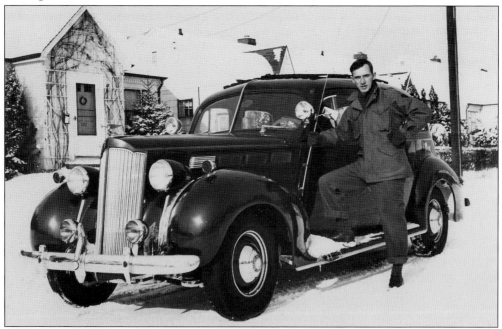

In this c. 1942 photograph, Jim Fitchett, a resident of Jefferson Street, is seen with his 1938 Packard Six automobile. This car was used for the two days before Christmas 1942 to deliver the Franklin Square parcel post mail because the regular US mail trucks were out of service at that time. This photograph was taken on Jefferson Street between Fenworth and Naple Avenues. As of 2001, Fitchett still owned this automobile; from time to time it was exhibited in local parades.

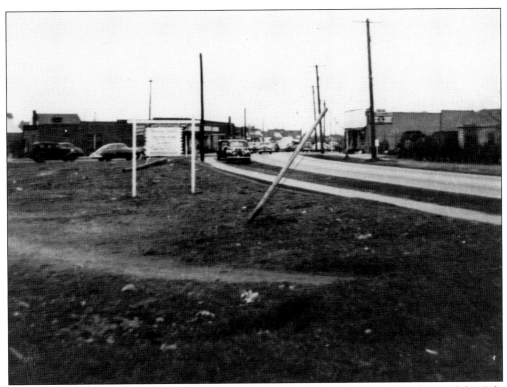

The site of the new Ascension Lutheran Church on Franklin Avenue is the subject of this July 1, 1950, photograph. The view is from the vacant land near Plane Avenue, looking south on Franklin Avenue. Note the sign at center announcing the site of the new edifice. Cars at left center are on Cloud Avenue. Note the narrowness of Franklin Avenue in 1950.

The Koke family of Franklin Square posed for a group photograph on their automobile in this 1928 snapshot. At lower right is Dorothy Koke Realmuto, a lifelong resident of Franklin Square. Like many Franklin Square families in the 1920s, the Kokes made good use of the automobile, which was becoming increasingly common and necessary for life in Nassau County. (Courtesy of Patricia Realmuto and Diane Serrapica.)

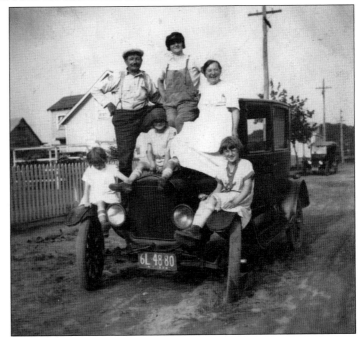

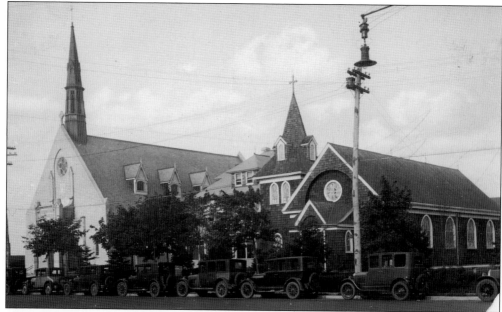

This photograph of St. Catherine of Sienna parish dates from 1926 or 1927. At left is the grand new church, completed in 1926. At center is the rectory, constructed in 1914. At right is old St. Catherine's, constructed when the parish was founded in 1908. This grouping of buildings endured from 1926 until 1931, when old St. Catherine's was moved down Lutz Street and became the American Legion Hall.

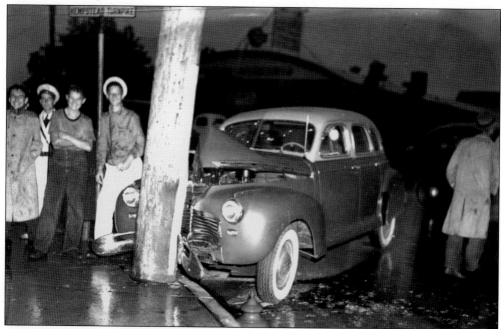

This 1941 photograph was taken just after an automobile accident at the east corner of Hempstead Turnpike and New Hyde Park Road. Note the wet road surface, the result of a rainstorm. The year of this photograph was ascertained by examining the license plate of the car damaged in the accident.

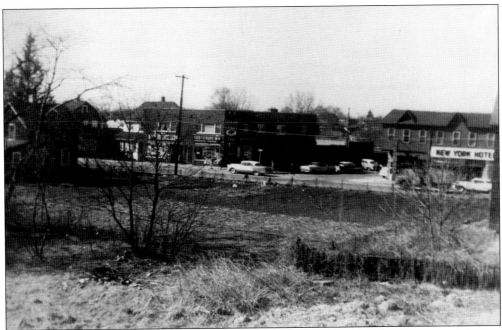

This is the Stevens Pansy Farm, a small field on New Hyde Park Road that was one of the last cultivated areas in Franklin Square. It was located on the east side of the road, just south of Washington Street. The side street at center is Lewiston Street. This photograph was taken shortly before the farm was sold in 1962.

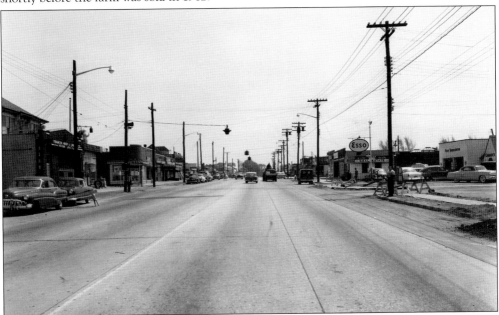

This photograph of Hempstead Turnpike, looking east, was taken about 1958 from a point just west of Commonwealth Street. Visible on the north side of the street (at left) is the old Munson firehouse and businesses, such as Riewerts and Lehmann Delicatessen and the Munson Bakery. At right is Charlie's Esso, at the corner of Commonwealth Street; Arthur's Liquor is at the corner of Rintin Street.

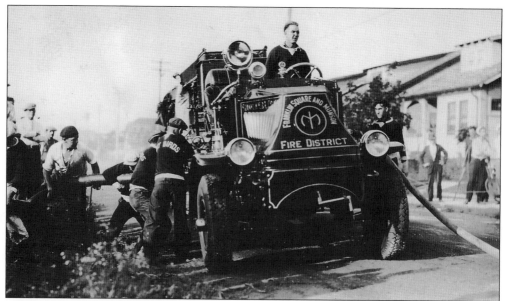

This picture illustrates the 1931 Franklin Square and Munson Fire Department tournament. The Sky Birds drill team is in the midst of an exercise at the corner of James Street and Benris Avenue (James Street is in the foreground). The view is looking north toward Hempstead Turnpike. Fire department events were an important part of community life in Franklin Square in the early 20th century.

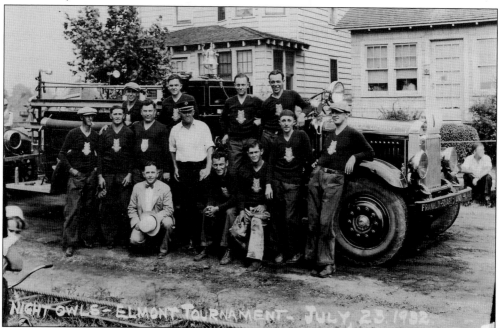

The Night Owls were the Franklin Square and Munson Fire Department Tournament Team. This photograph, taken on July 23, 1932, shows the Night Owls and the Franklin Square truck at the Elmont Fire Department Tournament at Elmont, Long Island. The tournament enabled local fireman to sharpen their skills, for there were relatively few fires in Franklin Square in the 1930s.

Six

RELIGIOUS LIFE

In the 19th century, there were no organized religious congregations in Franklin Square. The majority of residents, who were German-speaking Catholics, attended St. Boniface's Church in Foster's Meadow (present-day Elmont). German-speaking Protestants attended the German Presbyterian Church, also in Elmont. English-speaking residents favored the Methodist Church in Hempstead.

In 1908, the Catholics of Franklin Square decided to organize their own parish church and petitioned the bishop of Brooklyn for assistance. On July 5, 1908, Franklin Square celebrated its first mass in the front parlor of the old Kinsey Homestead. Within a year, St. Catherine of Sienna Church's chapel had been constructed on New Hyde Park Road. In 1913, Father Farrenkopf became the first resident priest. The parish grew quickly, and by 1926, the current Gothic church was completed.

The Protestant residents of Franklin Square, organized by Mrs. A. Fredericks, constructed St. James Episcopal Church in 1913. This was followed by the construction of Ascension Lutheran Church in 1923, the Orthodox Presbyterian Church in 1939, and the Wesley Methodist Church in 1947. In 1940, the Jewish community of Franklin Square organized the Franklin Square Jewish Center. The Jewish Center's current home on Pacific Street is the old St. Catherine's chapel. In 1956, the Bethel Assembly of God opened on Court House Road. Over the years, the religious congregations of Franklin Square have contributed greatly to the life of the community.

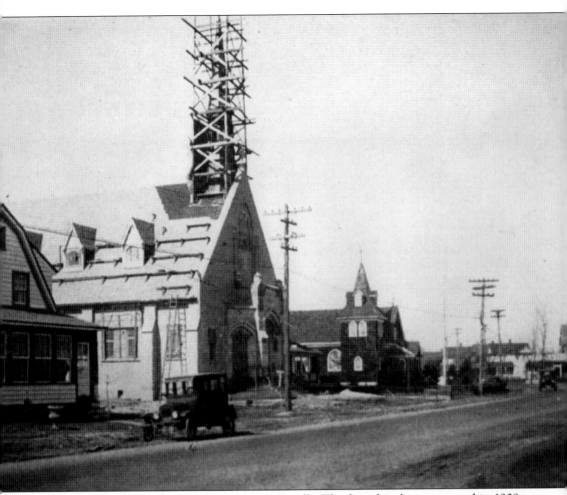

The parish of St. Catherine of Sienna grew rapidly. The first church, constructed in 1908, was already far too small just 15 years later. In 1913, the parish received its first resident priest. In 1917, Msgr. Conrad Lutz became pastor, a post he would hold until 1953. It was Monsignor Lutz who planned the new church, which would become one of the most beautiful public buildings in the area. The stained-glass windows, crafted in Germany to Monsignor Lutz's specifications, are unique works of art that illustrate the life of St. Catherine, patroness of Franklin Square. The altars, altar rail, and baptismal font are of white Italian marble. This photograph shows the church under construction in the winter of 1925–1926. Note the scaffolding around the steeple, roof, and stained-glass windows. Also visible is the rectory porch (to the immediate right of the new church) and old St. Catherine's at the center. The view is looking north from the east side of New Hyde Park Road.

This is a portrait of Fr. Augustus Rath, a Roman Catholic priest born in 1881 in Franklin Square. Father Rath walked three miles daily to St. Boniface's School in Elmont. In 1931, he became pastor of St. Boniface, a position he held until his death in 1948. Father Rath was the first priest born in Franklin Square.

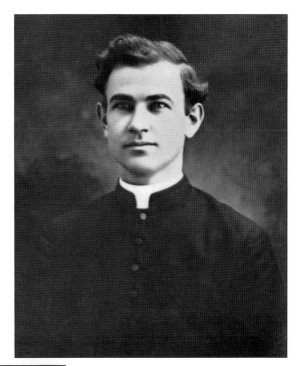

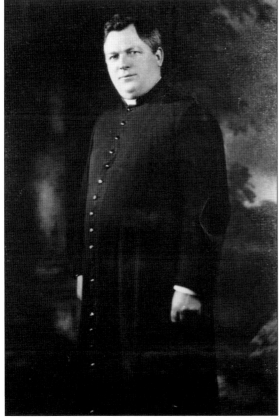

This is a portrait of Msgr. Conrad B. Lutz, pastor of St. Catherine of Sienna Church from 1917 to 1953. This image dates from the 1920s. Monsignor Lutz was responsible for the construction of the current St. Catherine of Sienna Church as well as the old Parish Hall. He also initiated the school building fund.

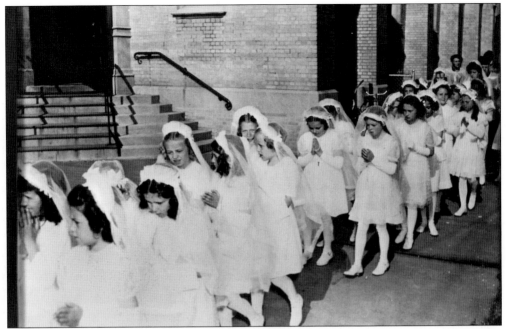

This c. 1947 photograph shows a St. Catherine of Sienna Church First Communion procession. Here, St. Catherine's First Communicants proceed from the rectory yard to the church to receive First Communion. At upper left are the church doors; at far right, behind the children, is Fr. Joseph Hack (with hat). Father Hack was Monsignor Lutz's assistant until 1948.

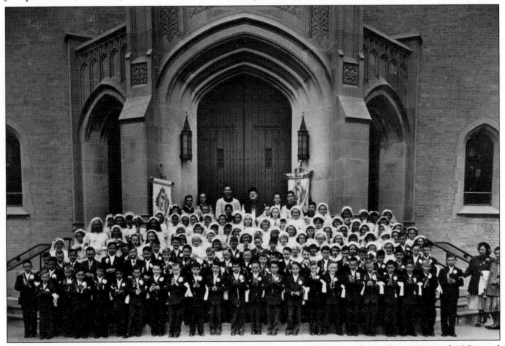

This image of a First Communion class at St. Catherine of Sienna dates from May of 1951 and was taken on the steps of the main church. In the center of the top row are Father Schlick (center left) and, directly to his right, Msgr. Conrad Lutz.

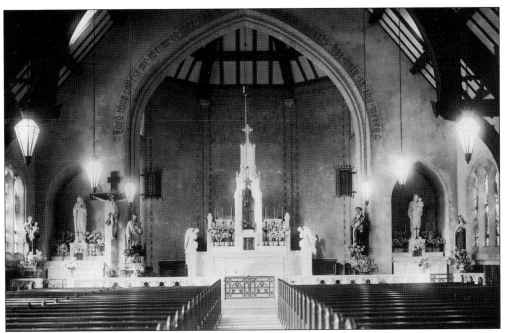

This photograph shows the interior of St. Catherine of Sienna Church as it appeared in 1943. The altars are of white Italian marble, and the magnificent stained-glass windows were crafted in Munich, Germany. The interior of St. Catherine's was remarkably similar nearly 70 years later, though the church has been periodically repainted in various colors.

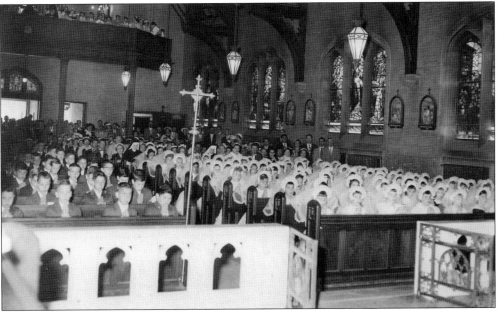

This photograph depicts the First Communion Mass in progress on May 30, 1958. This picture gives a fine view of the nave of St. Catherine of Sienna Church, rarely photographed from this angle. Note the original light fixtures (replaced in the 1970s); the wooden vaulting; the choir loft with its rose window depicting St. Cecilia, patroness of music; the altar rail (altered in 1991); and the bronze altar gates (removed in 1990).

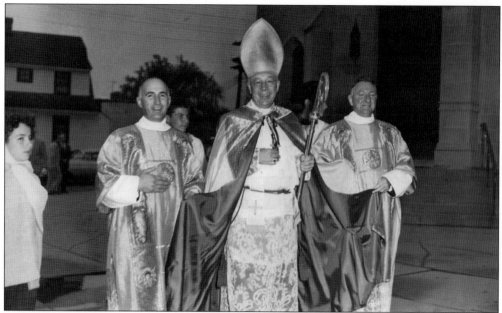

Here, Walter Kellenberg, bishop of Rockville Centre, is depicted returning to St. Catherine of Sienna Church's Rectory after administering the Sacrament of Confirmation on June 10, 1958. Bishop Kellenberg is dressed in full regalia—including miter, crozier, and cope—for the procession to the rectory. Accompanying Bishop Kellenberg at left is Father Melton (formerly of St. Catherine's). This photograph was taken on the sidewalk in front of St. Catherine of Sienna Church.

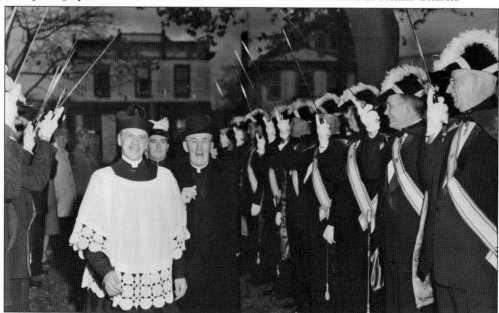

On November 11, 1956, Auxiliary Bishop of Brooklyn Edmund J. Reilly visited St. Catherine of Sienna Church in order to dedicate the school auditorium and to administer the Sacrament of Confirmation. In this picture, Fr. Anthony Holzheimer (left) meets Bishop Reilly (right) in front of St. Catherine of Sienna Church's Rectory. The local Knights of Columbus chapter provided an honor guard for His Excellency.

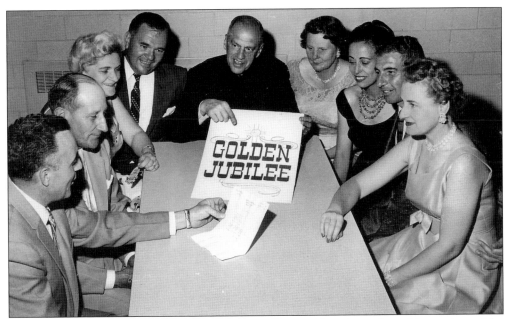

Here, Father Holzheimer, pastor of St. Catherine of Sienna Church, confers with members of the parish Golden Jubilee Committee. Father Holzheimer points to an artist's layout of the Golden Jubilee logo. Among those at the table were William Hoffman (an original parishioner, second from left); Pat DiGiovanna (third from left); Peter Meyer (fourth from left); Father Holzheimer (center); and Howard Allum (second from right).

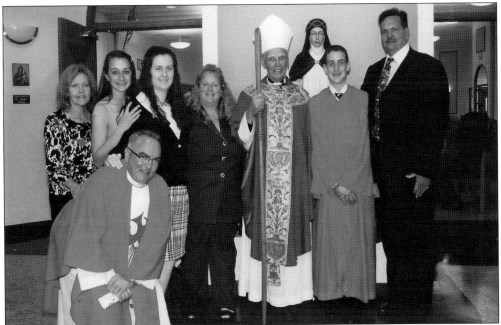

This April 2010 picture was taken at St. Catherine of Sienna Church on Confirmation Day. Pictured are Bishop Paul H. Walsh (center) and Fr. Ed Sheridan (front left), along with the Mutum family. Traditionally, this sacrament is held once a year when the bishop confirms the youth of the parish.

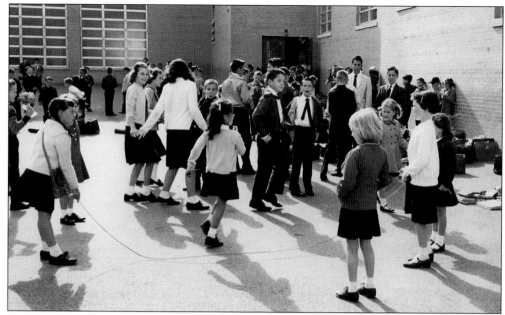

Students await the start of the school day in the St. Catherine of Sienna School yard in 1958. Schoolbooks have been placed against the wall at right. The view is looking east in the portion of the school yard between the school and the convent. The large windows at left are those of the school auditorium.

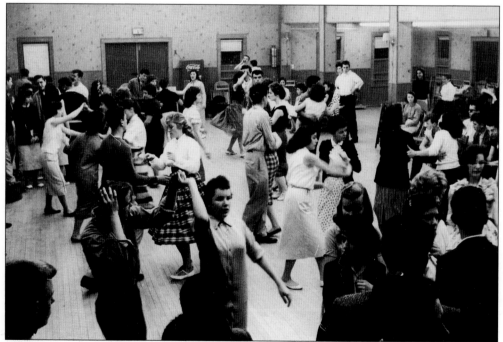

This 1958 image shows teenagers dancing at St. Catherine's Senior High Confraternity. After the discussion portion of the evening, a social hour or dance followed. The activities took place in St. Catherine of Sienna Church's spacious old Parish Hall, which served as the Kalb Hotel horse barn until 1920.

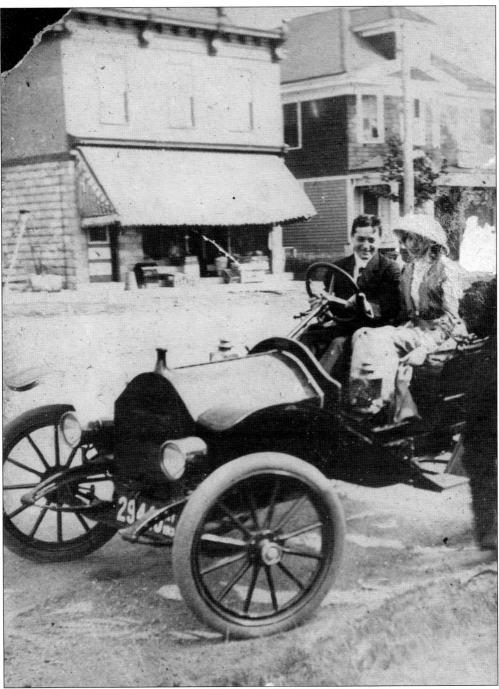

This August 26, 1913, photograph shows a young couple leaving the wedding ceremonies at St. Catherine of Sienna Church. They are parked at the present-day corner of New Hyde Park Road and Lutz Street. Across New Hyde Park Road is Gaetano Re's store, opened the previous year, and to the right of it is Thomala's Butcher Shop. In 1913, New Hyde Park Road, a broad thoroughfare, was considered to be the main street of Franklin Square. This is an interesting picture of an early automobile; in 1913, the horse and buggy was still in general use in Franklin Square.

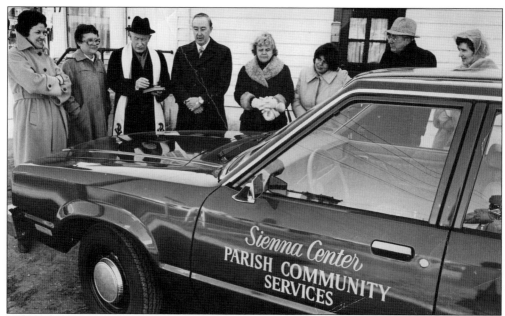

The Sienna Center is a social outreach program founded by St. Catherine of Sienna Church in the late 1970s. In this February 29, 1980, photograph, the Ridgewood Savings Bank presents a new station wagon to assist the elderly and infirm. Among those pictured are Fr. S. Thomas Minogue (third from left); Sr. Jeanne Andre Brendel, O.P., (second from left); and Eugene Murphy of the Ridgewood Savings Bank (fourth from left).

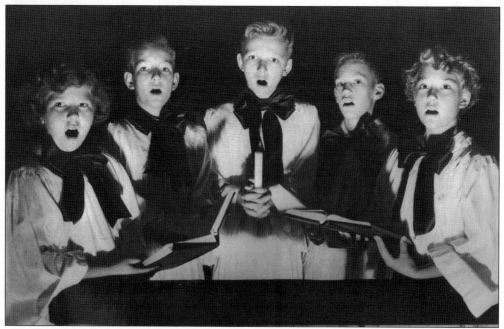

The St. Andrew's children's choir is the subject of this photograph from the late 1950s. The children are singing in the sanctuary of the old section of the church on Nassau Boulevard. Although St. Andrew's is located in the West Hempstead postal area, it is actually in the Franklin Square School District.

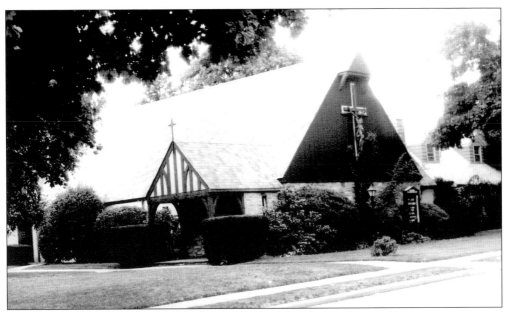

This is a view of St. James the Just Episcopal Church taken on Roosevelt Street, just east of Monroe Street. Constructed in 1955 and 1956 using wood and stone in an English rural Gothic style, the building is known for its massive crucifix facing Roosevelt Street. St. James' rectory is at far right. The congregation closed its doors early in 2011.

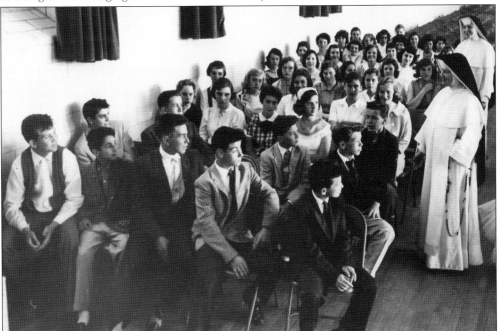

This is a view of St. Catherine's Senior High Confraternity in the school auditorium in 1958. Senior public school students attended the program on Wednesday evenings, while the younger students attended on Saturday mornings. Enrolled in the Confraternity program in 1958 were 1,222 students. Here, Sr. M. Catherine William (front), first principal of St. Catherine of Sienna School, and Sr. Mary Jeremy (back) speak with Confraternity students.

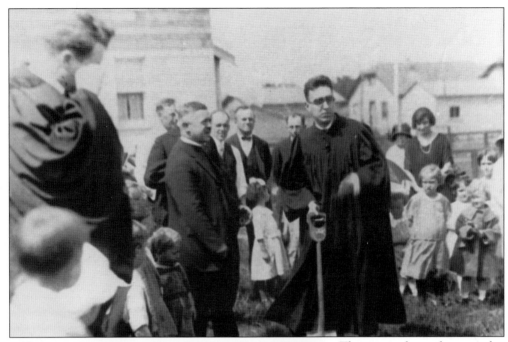

This image shows the ground breaking for the original Ascension Lutheran Church on May 31, 1925. Located at the corner of Court House Road and Washington Street, the building is now Bethel Assembly of God Church. Three pastors are shown here: Moldenke, Burke, and Luther Gerhart at the shovel. In the picture are onlookers Mr. Hubley, Mr. Elson, Mrs. Davidson, Marie Endres, and Cathy Major.

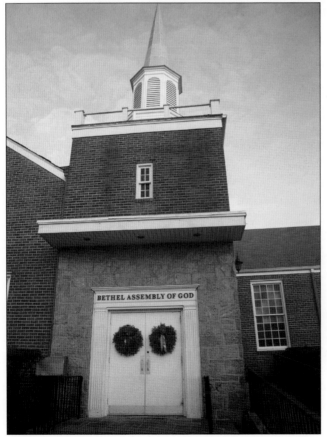

The Bethel Assembly of God congregation moved into the old Ascension Lutheran Church building in the 1950s. The congregation enlarged the former Lutheran church with a new wing along Washington Street. A large steeple was added in the 1960s. This view is from the northeast corner of Washington Street and Court House Road.

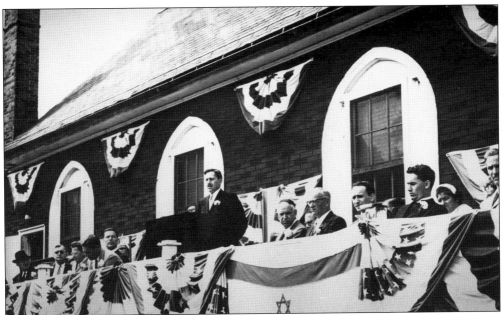

The Franklin Square Jewish Center was founded in 1940. In 1942, the center brought the old American Legion Hall (formerly St. Catherine's original church) on Pacific Street. In 1955, the center broke ground for a new addition. This photograph was taken at the ground-breaking ceremony; the dais was set up along the original building. On the dais are various community leaders, clergymen, and members of the Jewish Center Congregation.

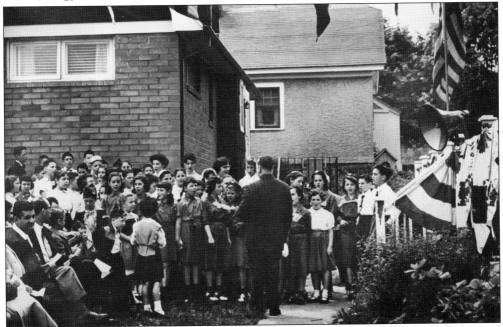

This photograph, taken at the 1955 Franklin Square Jewish Center addition ground-breaking ceremony, shows the Brownie and Girl Scout troops affiliated with the center's Hebrew School. A large population of children, as evidenced here, was one of the motivating forces in the expansion of the center. The photograph looks westward from the center's grounds along Lloyd Street.

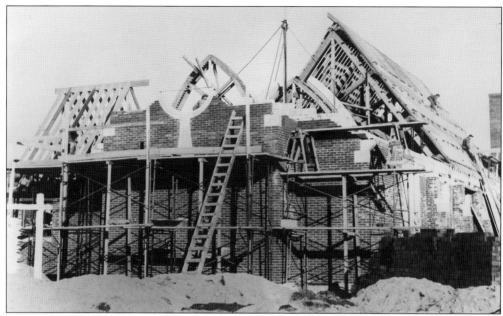

A 1950 photograph shows Ascension Lutheran Church under construction. The view is looking east toward the construction site. This is the Ascension Lutheran building that is in use today. Ascension Lutheran Church was organized in the old Scheld House on Ascension Eve in 1923. It was the third religious congregation organized in Franklin Square.

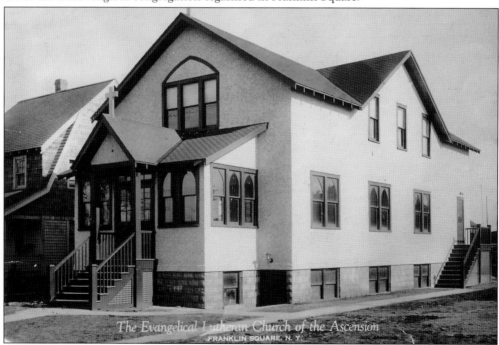

The original Ascension Lutheran Church was located on the northeast corner of Court House Road and Washington Street. Built in 1925, the original edifice was both church and parsonage. This picture shows the newly built church as it appeared in the winter of 1925–1926. Ascension remained in this location until the early 1950s.

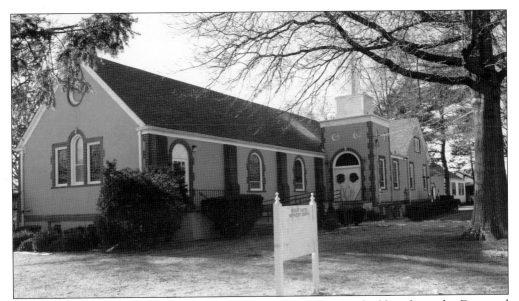

Wesley United Methodist Church was organized in 1947. The present building, located at Dogwood Avenue and Fenworth Boulevard, was constructed in 1948. The parsonage was completed in 1950. This view of the church was taken from a point near the corner of Dogwood Avenue and Fenworth Boulevard. Wesley Methodist Church boasts a number of beautiful stained-glass windows.

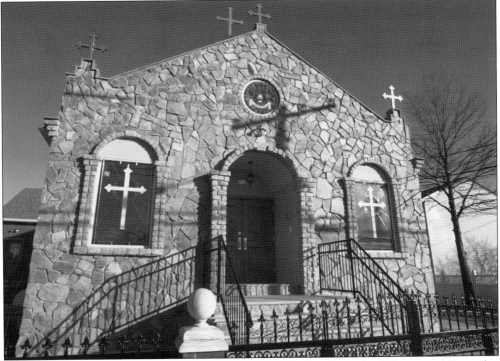

St. Basil Orthodox Church is located on Randolph Avenue, just south of Hempstead Turnpike. St. Basil is housed in the former American Legion Hall, originally constructed in the 1940s. The American Legion Post sold the building, which was subsequently renovated into the present church. St. Basil is the newest religious congregation in Franklin Square.

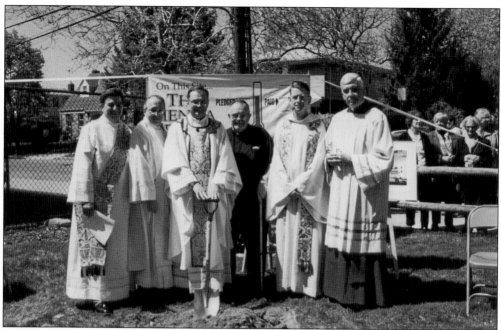

After the closure of the old parish hall in the 1990s, St. Catherine of Sienna parish urgently needed space for its numerous activities. Beginning in 2000, Msgr. Thomas Groenewold led the efforts to build a new parish facility—the Sienna Center—that would house a chapel and meeting rooms. Above, Monsignor Groenewold is at center with shovel. The facility was completed in 2004 and the dedication Mass held on June 7 of that year. Below, Monsignor Groenewold is shown with the parish's deacons at the dedication Mass. The Sienna Center has proved to be an invaluable addition to the spiritual and social life of Franklin Square. (Courtesy of Robert Murawski.)

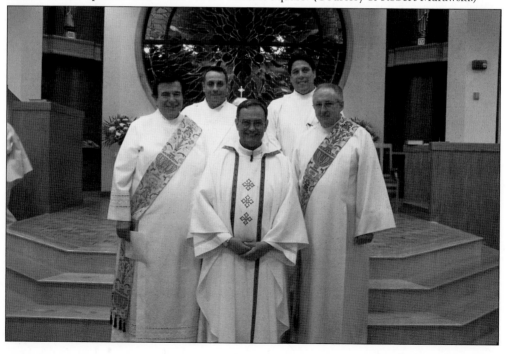

Seven

PRIDE AND PATRIOTISM

Franklin Square residents have always been proud of their community and their nation. Lauritz Nelson, a well-known veteran, was awarded the Congressional Medal of Honor for his service in the Spanish-American War of 1898. Local men served in World War I, and their homecoming celebration was a memorable event in local history. American Legion and VFW Posts were set up in Franklin Square after World War I, and ever since, they have assisted our veterans while promoting the ideals of democracy and patriotism. During World War II, the people of Franklin Square constructed a large Honor Roll in the middle of town, listing every local resident serving in the armed forces. In 1938, Franklin Square unveiled a permanent veterans' monument honoring the veterans of all US conflicts. This monument, now located in Rath Park, is the focal point of the annual Memorial Day parade.

In recent years, Franklin Square continues to remember seven local residents killed in the attacks of September 11, 2001. A monument to their memories stands near the Victorian Gazebo on Naple Avenue.

One of Franklin Square's proudest days in recent years was a homecoming parade in honor of Michael Massimino, a Franklin Square resident who orbited the earth in the space shuttle.

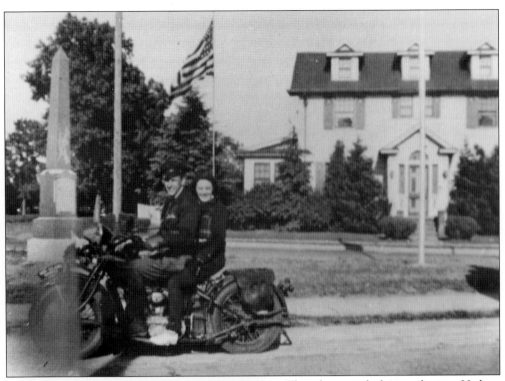

This photograph depicts the new Hyde Park and Court House Road corner as it appeared on Memorial Day in 1938. Shown is the newly erected monument, now on Naple Avenue in Rath Park. This was the dedication day for the veterans' monument. At rear is Andrew Hoffman's home, built around 1923. The house has since been remodeled and is now the Franklin Funeral Home.

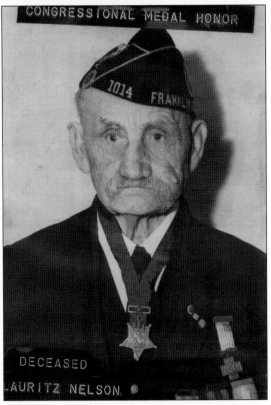

Lauritz Nelson (1858–1941), a Franklin Square resident, was a winner of the Congressional Medal of Honor for his role in the Spanish-American War. He was a member of American Legion Post 1014 and affiliated with the VFW as well. For many years, this photograph was displayed in the Legion Hall on Pacific Street and later in the newer building on Randolph Avenue.

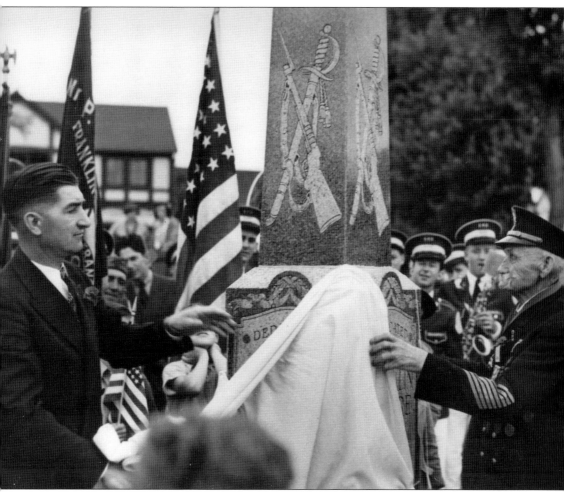

This close-up view of the dedication ceremonies for the Franklin Square veterans' monument dates from Memorial Day 1938. At left is John E. Rath, civic leader, and at right is Lauritz Nelson, recipient of the Congressional Medal of Honor. The monument, originally located at the corner of Court House and New Hyde Park Roads, is now at Rath Park.

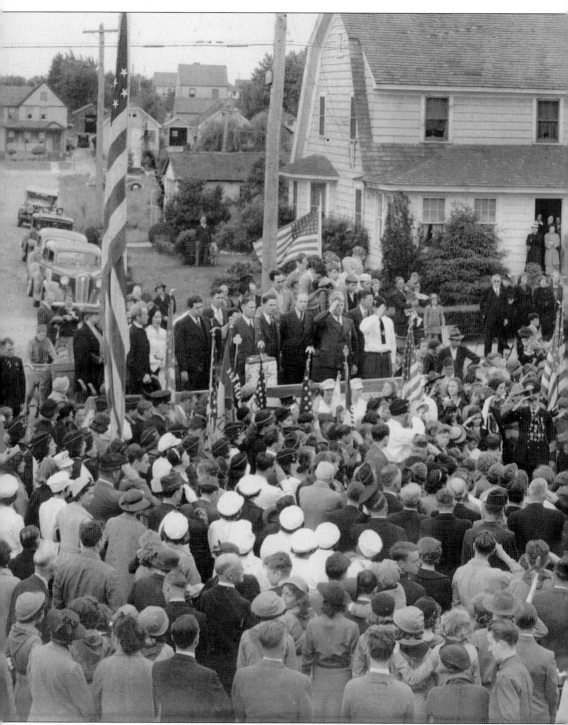

The Franklin Square veterans' monument was dedicated on Memorial Day 1938. John Rath, local civic leader, coordinated the drive to design and purchase the granite obelisk. The original site of the monument, as shown in this dedication scene, was located at the triangular junction of Court House and New Hyde Park Roads. A large crowd turned out to witness the dedication ceremonies,

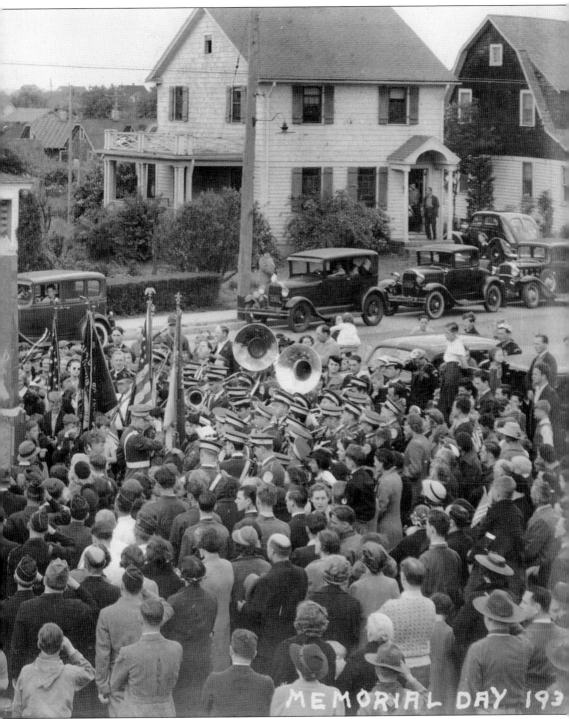

MEMORIAL DAY 193

which were led by veteran Lauritz Nelson, along with John Rath. This photograph was taken from the upper story of today's Franklin Funeral Home, looking west across Court House Road. Two decades later, the monument was moved to a new site at Rath Park on Naple Avenue.

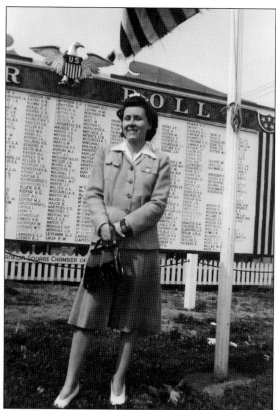

Josephine Moren, a longtime resident of Franklin Square (1920s–2000s), poses in front of the Franklin Square Honor Roll in this photograph from 1943. The Honor Roll, erected to honor local men serving in the armed forces during World War II, was set up on Hempstead Turnpike. There were several hundred names on the list. At left, the donor's name, the Franklin Square Chamber of Commerce, is partially visible.

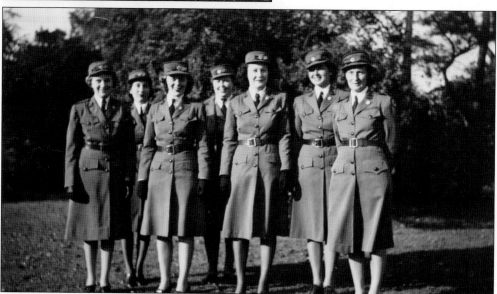

From 1943 to 1945, Helen E. Quinn of Monroe Street was a volunteer ambulance driver at Mitchell Field. This October 21, 1945, photograph was taken at the Nassau Hospital Rally on the grounds of the Cathedral of the Incarnation in Garden City. Pictured here are, from left to right, Helen E. Quinn, Mary Tabacoff, Hazel Schmidt, Ethel Buch, Jennie Rigberg, Betty Vrektry, and Florence Carpenter (dispatcher).

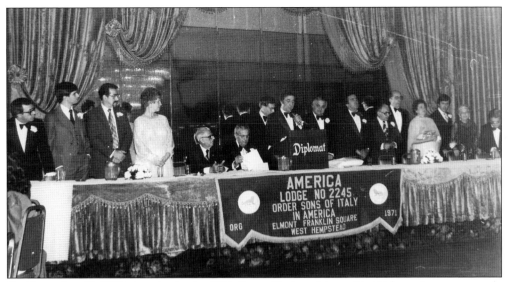

On November 15, 1980, America Lodge 2245, Sons of Italy, celebrated its 10th anniversary at a gala scholarship dinner dance at the Diplomat Catering Hall in Franklin Square. In this photograph, chairman Joseph DiGennaro introduces the guest of honor, ex-Venerable Sal Palmeri. (Courtesy of the Sons of Italy, America Lodge 2245.)

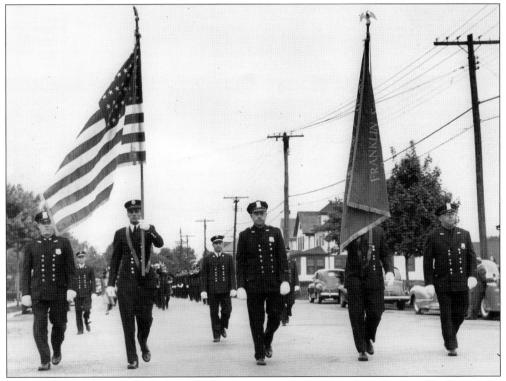

The Franklin Square and Munson Fire Department is pictured in this photograph taken at the 1948 Memorial Day parade. The fire department has traditionally formed a major component of the parade. Here, the fire department's color guard is followed by the firemen and a band hired for the occasion. The parade is proceeding along Herman Boulevard.

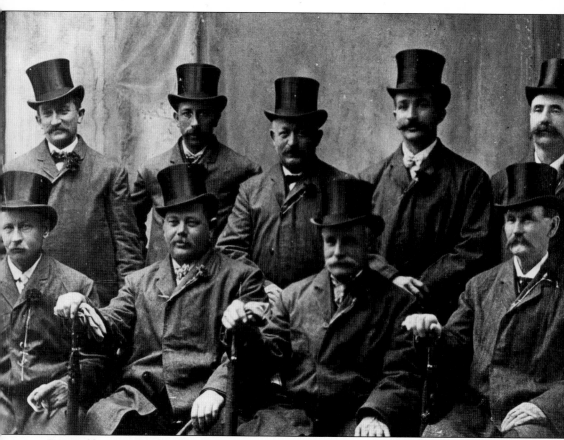

Pictured here are Franklin Square citizens at Theodore Roosevelt's inauguration on March 4, 1905. In 1904, Theodore Roosevelt, the only president to call Nassau County home, was elected to the presidency. Many Nassau County Republicans and friends were invited to attend the inauguration proceedings in Washington, DC. Among them were nine Franklin Square citizens, pictured here, from left to right, as follows: (first row) John Kiefer, August Pfalzer, W.S. Stringham, and Herman A. Utz; (second row) Peter J. Herman, Peter Kinsey, Jacob Hoffman, Seaman Elderd, and John Hoffman. The gentlemen were invited to march in the Inaugural Parade and were also invited to a gala "Dinner in Honor of President's Neighbors" held at a Washington hotel. This souvenir photograph was taken in Washington.

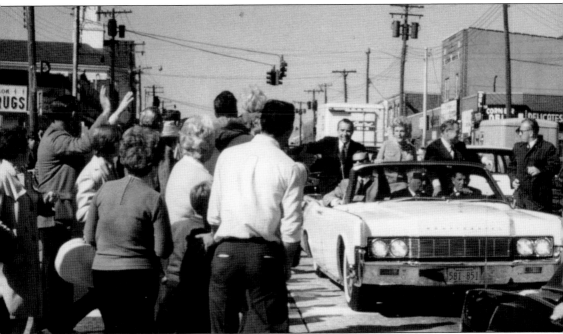

This photograph dates from the presidential campaign of 1968. On October 5, 1968, candidate (later president) Richard M. Nixon passed through Franklin Square on his way to a campaign rally coordinated by the Nassau County Republican Committee. Nixon's motorcade stopped briefly on Hempstead Turnpike in front of the Franklin Square Post Office, where the candidate said a few words. In the car were Richard Nixon, Pat Nixon, Gov. Nelson Rockefeller, and Margaretta "Happy" Rockefeller. Later, in October 1968, Democratic presidential candidate Hubert Humphrey also stopped briefly at the same place. Since the late 1800s, Franklin Square has almost always supported Republican candidates for practically every level of elected office. Over the years, many candidates for the presidency have passed through Franklin Square. John F. Kennedy, for example, did so in 1960. As New York is no longer a contested state in most presidential elections, candidates no longer regularly visit.

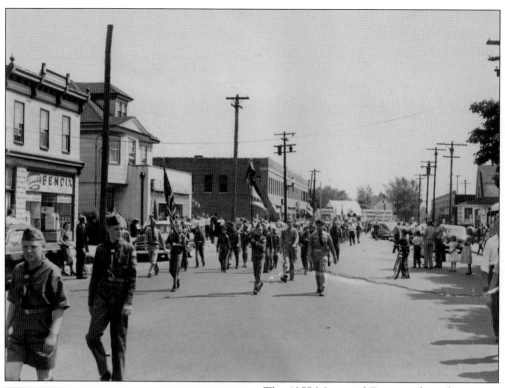

The 1955 Memorial Day parade makes its way northward on New Hyde Park Road in this photograph. Prior to 1960, Memorial Day parades ended at the veterans' monument at the corner of Court House and New Hyde Park Roads. The route was changed with the relocation of the monument to Rath Park.

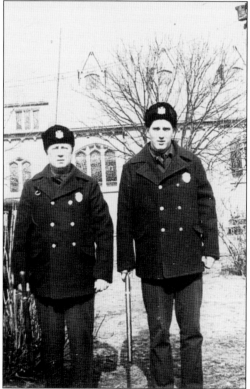

James Mott (left) and Daniel Mott were both members of the Nassau County Auxiliary Police. The Motts are shown in their uniforms in this photograph from the late 1940s. The view was taken on Holzheimer Street just west of New Hyde Park Road, with the south facade of St. Catherine of Sienna Church serving as a backdrop.

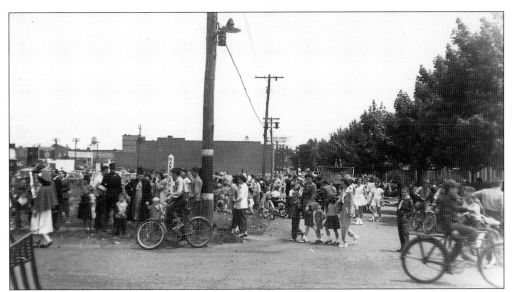

This photograph shows the assembly point of the 1949 Memorial Day parade at the corner of Randolph and Phoebe Streets. This photograph is interesting in that it shows the large lot that was the future site of Woolworth's. Beyond is the heart of downtown area. Also note the old-style light fixture on the pole at center; such fixtures remained until the 1960s.

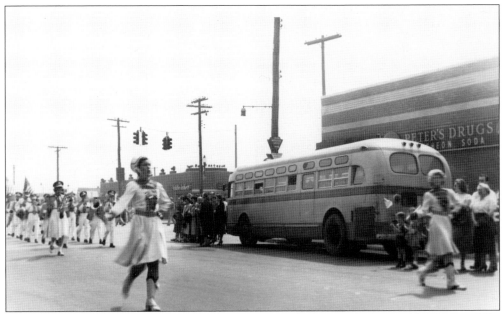

This photograph was taken during the 1950 Memorial Day parade in Franklin Square. The location is the intersection of New Hyde Park Road and Hempstead Turnpike. At left is a store that was, for many years, the location of Dellerson Drugs; here, the sign advertises "Peter's Drugs: Luncheon Soda." In the 1950s, the parade ended at the corner of Court House and New Hyde Park Roads.

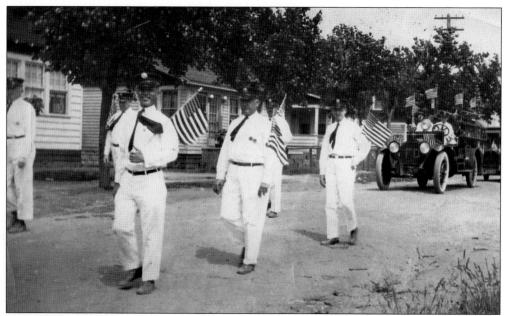

Here, the Franklin Square and Munson Fire Department is on parade. Some of the early fire trucks are bringing up the rear. The picture is believed to be of the annual parade of firemen in Floral Park on August 1, 1925. The Franklin Square Fire Department traces its beginnings to 1907 when a group of local farmers organized the Munson volunteer group.

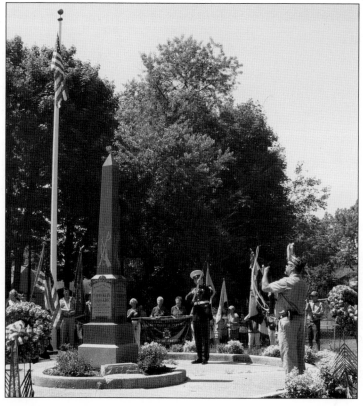

In the 21st century, Franklin Square continues to observe patriotic traditions established generations ago. One of these traditions is the annual Memorial Day celebration, which has changed little over the years. The day begins with a parade down Hempstead Turnpike from the VFW Hall to the veterans' monument in Rath Park, where wreaths are presented and tributes rendered. This photograph shows members of the VFW Ladies Auxiliary and a Marine during the 2010 ceremony. (Courtesy of Carol Grassi.)

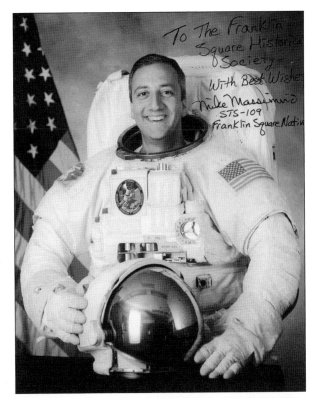

Michael Massimino, who spent his early life in Franklin Square, was selected by NASA to serve as an astronaut. Involved in a number of challenging missions, Massimino has maintained ties with his hometown. Franklin Square held a memorable homecoming parade in his honor in 2002. On June 11, 2004, Massimino visited John Street School. Here, Massimino presents NASA patches to Evan and Kiera Grassi as Principal Ceil Candreva looks on. (Courtesy of Carol Grassi.)

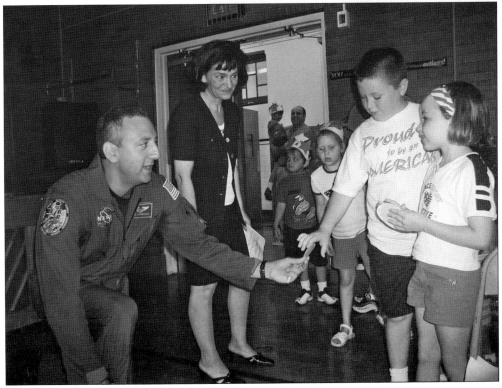

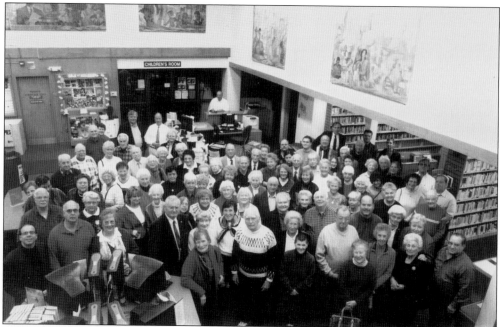

This group photograph was taken on March 11, 2004, as the official silver anniversary photograph of the Franklin Square Historical Society. The members were assembled in the main room of the Franklin Square Library. Note the murals, belonging to the society, on the upper walls of the room. These murals were originally in the consumer lobby of the Franklin National Bank.

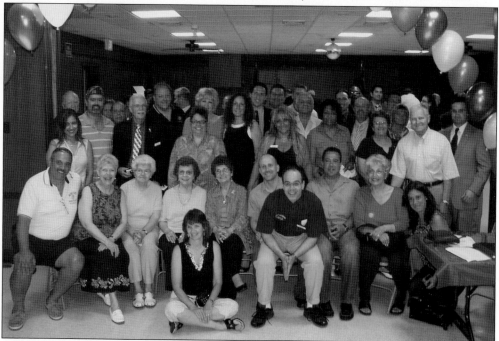

The business community of Franklin Square is represented by the Franklin Square of Chamber of Commerce. The chamber of commerce has been active for over 60 years. This photograph of the chamber was taken at the June 24, 2010, meeting held at the VFW Hall on Lincoln Road.

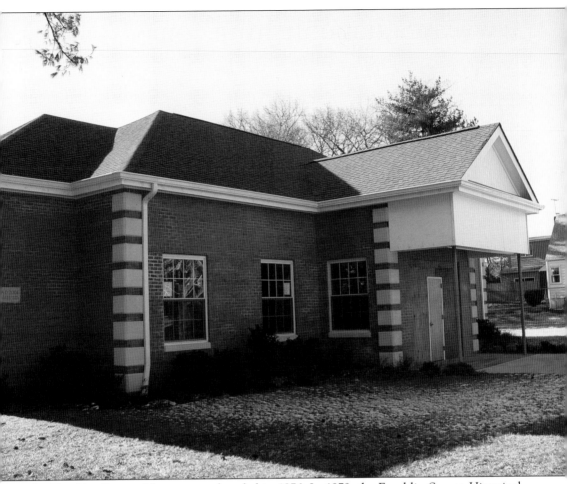

The Franklin Square Museum was founded in 1976. In 1979, the Franklin Square Historical Society was founded to support and operate the museum, which was originally located in John Street School. In 1993, the society voted to construct its own museum building, and by 2001, the architectural plans were drawn. This photograph depicts the Georgian facade of the building, which was constructed in 2006 on Naple Avenue at Rath Park. All of the author's royalties from the sales of this book will be devoted to completing the building's interior. The Franklin Square Historical Society looks forward to sharing its many treasures with the public upon completion of the building. Girl Scouts and coauthors Kiera Grassi and Hannah Mutum took this picture on January 10, 2010 (1-10-10, which is also the Franklin Square zip code, 11010), as part of a photographic survey of the village.

www.arcadiapublishing.com

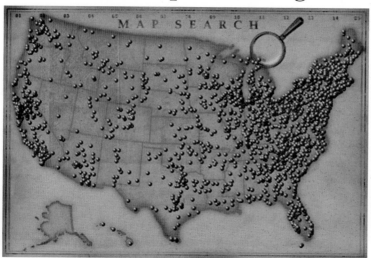

MAP SEARCH

Discover books about the town where you grew up, the cities where your friends and families live, the town where your parents met, or even that retirement spot you've been dreaming about. Our Web site provides history lovers with exclusive deals, advanced notification about new titles, e-mail alerts of author events, and much more.

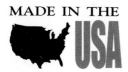

MADE IN THE USA

Arcadia Publishing, the leading local history publisher in the United States, is committed to making history accessible and meaningful through publishing books that celebrate and preserve the heritage of America's people and places. Consistent with our mission to preserve history on a local level, this book was printed in South Carolina on American-made paper and manufactured entirely in the United States.

This book carries the accredited Forest Stewardship Council (FSC) label and is printed on 100 percent FSC-certified paper. Products carrying the FSC label are independently certified to assure consumers that they come from forests that are managed to meet the social, economic, and ecological needs of present and future generations.

FSC
Mixed Sources
Product group from well-managed
forests and other controlled sources
Cert no. SW-COC-001530
www.fsc.org
© 1996 Forest Stewardship Council

Find Your Place in History.